Rose Colored Glass

by Susan Bigelow
and Janice Goldberg

A Samuel French Acting Edition

New York Hollywood London Toronto
SAMUELFRENCH.COM

Copyright © 1999, 2007 by Susan Bigelow and Janice Goldberg

ALL RIGHTS RESERVED

CAUTION: Professionals and amateurs are hereby warned that *ROSE COLORED GLASS* are subject to a Licensing Fee. It is fully protected under the copyright laws of the United States of America, the British Commonwealth, including Canada, and all other countries of the Copyright Union. All rights, including professional, amateur, motion picture, recitation, lecturing, public reading, radio broadcasting, television and the rights of translation into foreign languages are strictly reserved. In its present form the play is dedicated to the reading public only.

The amateur live stage performance rights to *ROSE COLORED GLASS* are controlled exclusively by Samuel French, Inc., and licensing arrangements and performance licenses must be secured well in advance of presentation. PLEASE NOTE that amateur Licensing Fees are set upon application in accordance with your producing circumstances. When applying for a licensing quotation and a performance license please give us the number of performances intended, dates of production, your seating capacity and admission fee. Licensing Fees are payable one week before the opening performance of the play to Samuel French, Inc., at 45 W. 25th Street, New York, NY 10010.

Licensing Fee of the required amount must be paid whether the play is presented for charity or gain and whether or not admission is charged.

Stock licensing fees quoted upon application to Samuel French, Inc.

For all other rights than those stipulated above, apply to: Samuel French, Inc., at 45 W. 25th Street, New York, NY 10010.

Particular emphasis is laid on the question of amateur or professional readings, permission and terms for which must be secured in writing from Samuel French, Inc.

Copying from this book in whole or in part is strictly forbidden by law, and the right of performance is not transferable.

Whenever the play is produced the following notice must appear on all programs, printing and advertising for the play: "Produced by special arrangement with Samuel French, Inc."

Due authorship credit must be given on all programs, printing and advertising for the play.

ISBN 978-0-573-65080-2   Printed in U.S.A.   #20711

No one shall commit or authorize any act or omission by which the copyright of, or the right to copyright, this play may be impaired.

No one shall make any changes in this play for the purpose of production.

Publication of this play does not imply availability for performance. Both amateurs and professionals considering a production are strongly advised in their own interests to apply to Samuel French, Inc., for written permission before starting rehearsals, advertising, or booking a theatre.

No part of this book may be reproduced, stored in a retrieval system, or transmitted in any form, by any means, now known or yet to be invented, including mechanical, electronic, photocopying, recording, videotaping, or otherwise, without the prior written permission of the publisher.

IMPORTANT BILLING AND CREDIT REQUIREMENTS

All producers of *ROSE COLORED GLASS must* give credit to the Author of the Play in all programs distributed in connection with performances of the Play, and in all instances in which the title of the Play appears for the purposes of advertising, publicizing or otherwise exploiting the Play and/or a production. The name of the Author *must* appear on a separate line on which no other name appears, immediately following the title and *must* appear in size of type not less than fifty percent of the size of the title type.

ROSE COLORED GLASS had its premiere at Theatre 54@Shetler Studios in May, 2007 in New York City and was presented by GalCo Productions, in association with Shetler Studios Theatrical Development Groups. The set was designed by Chad M. Brinkman. The lighting was designed by Robin A. Paterson. The costumes were designed by Debra Otte. Original music by Peter Yonka; Sound design by Craig Lenti. The prodution was directed by Janice Goldberg with the following cast:

LADY	Anita Keal
ROSE	Emily Zacharias
PEG	Brianne Moncrief

Special thanks to Michael Mullins and to Plays-In-Progress and North Coast Repertory Theatre in Northern California for their help in the development of this play.

CHARACTERS

LADY O'RILEY: 60's, Irish Catholic immigrant, owner of Lady O'Riley's Pub, church going, God fearing, has a natural warmth to her although is often irritable, feisty, raising her granddaugher, has spent her life working hard, stubborn, set in her ways. She is an idealist, believing that things will happen if you just have enough faith.

ROSE FLEISHMAN: late 40's, Austrian Jewish immigrant, widow, no children, owner of Fleishman's Delicatessen across the alley from the Pub, stoic, reserved, proud, doesn't let her guard down until the end, stubborn, set in her ways. She is more of a realist than Lady, and believes everything is a result of hard work, and even that sometimes is not enough.

PEG O'RILEY: 13 at the start of the play. Lady's granddaughter, intrigued by Rose, can be a little conniver and a bit of a smart aleck but there is a sweetness there. Is moving from childhood to awakening adolescence, attracted by things and people who are different, also stubborn, has a mission to get these women to become friends. She is fresh faced with an all-American look circa 1938. As the narrator, she is a bit older, and a bit wiser.

LOCATION

The action of the play takes place in Chicago in the back kitchens of Lady's Pub and Rose's Deli and in the alley that separates them. The time spans 1938-39.

AUTHORS' NOTE

Peg's monologues should be spoken from the viewpoint of the somewhat older, narrator Peg. There is also humor in this play that should not be shied away from.

Peg's monologues were written with the idea that they might be accompanied by visuals, that serve as a pictorial history of the events to which she refers. Also perhaps, to be accompanied by music. A series of pictures of children of the war close the show. Some of these pictures can be obtained from the United States Holocaust Memorial Museum.

ACT I

(The action takes place in the back rooms of LADY O'RILEY'S Pub and ROSE FLEISHMAN'S Delicatessen. ROSE'S kitchen contains a work table and chairs as well as a small table with a music box on it. LADY'S contains a tall work table, a counter and stools as well as a small table with tea service on it. There is a picture of Paddy on the wall. Both kitchens are equipped with stoves, refrigerators, and so on. Both contain a door that leads to the alley. The buildings are separated by that alley... It is Chicago, 1938.

PEG ENTERS and sits downstage in the alley on a crate and watches the action. ROSE, late 40's, ENTERS the alley, goes to her mailbox and removes a letter. LADY, early 60's, is bringing in a delivery. They purposely do not speak and each returns to her own kitchen. Music from the mid-30's fades into a more classical sound of Vienna as the following is heard. Lights fade up on ROSE'S kitchen. ROSE is sitting at the table with the letter.)

ROSE. *(Reading.)* April 30, 1938. My Dearest Rose. Life in Vienna is becoming more difficult by the day... the new Nazi government has required all Jews to register as such... and laws are being enacted that restrict Karl from taking anyone other than Jews as patients, cutting his practice by three quarters. I

ROSE COLORED GLASS

fear it won't be long before the tradesmen will be robbed of their livelihood as well. And as if that is not enough, Karl and I were forced to clean the streets... on our hands and knees... Many have been arrested and I fear for... Papa is feeling fine though, and insists that I write you shouldn't worry. He says it will pass. Love, Sabina.

(Lights come up on the alley. PEG goes and looks in the deli's mail box, and then looks in the pub's. SHE removes the mail, then speaks to the audience.)

PEG. That is how it all began... a trickle of information from across the world. When this story began, I was all of 13. It is a story that will be remembered as theirs, sometimes theirs alone, but sometimes as belonging to us all. It was a story to which we all thought we knew the ending... and, thus, the mistake began. *(Pause.)* On the stockyard side of Chicago... where the wind blows the 'wrong' way... on the corner of 71st and Colefax was my Grandmother's Pub and Grill. My Grandfather had died at an early age, and over the years O'Riley's had become Lady O'Riley's. It was July 1, 1938. For the young Jewish boys across town it was a year of Bar Mitzvahs. But on this side of the alley, becoming 13 was not so easy... no one wanted to consider *me* an adult. It was a time of questioning... a time of... unanswered questions. It seemed like the whole world was struggling to grow up. *(Pause.)* 1938... A year when the events of the world, the tension in Europe, the economy and the unrest in all our hearts seemed to melt together... the one thing for sure, however, was you could tell the day of the week by my grandmother's...

ROSE COLORED GLASS

(PEG ENTERS LADY'S kitchen through the alley door.)

    PEG. *(Cont'd.)* Blue Plate Special...

(PEG plops herself on the counter.)

    LADY. Off the counter.
    PEG. We got a letter for Mrs. Fleishman again...
    LADY. Put it in her box, child. Now, off the counter.

(PEG deliberately sets the letter next to her on counter.)

    PEG. Why? You're not doing anything on it.
    LADY. I could be. Off.
    PEG. *(Starts to head out to the alley.)* Can I...
    LADY. No... the tables have yet to be wiped down. And I want you to eat before you go running off...
    PEG. Nanna, it's a holiday weekend...
    LADY. I still want you to eat.
    PEG. Ah, Nanna, it's Friday.
    LADY. Soon there'll be a whole pub full of good Irish lads who have nothin' but the highest regards for my Salmon Loaf, and all I hear out of you is... Nanna, it's Friday.
    PEG. I could eat at the deli. That's still eating.
    LADY. That's a matter of opinion.
    PEG. Please.
    LADY. No. You eat over there far too often. You're gonna turn into one of them Gefilte fishes. You don't even know what's in it.
    PEG. It's fish. Isn't that all that counts... I mean, in God's eyes and all?

ROSE COLORED GLASS

LADY. What is it you don't like about my Salmon Loaf?
PEG. Nothing. It's just that we have it a lot.
LADY. That's why it's called a Blue Plate Special.
PEG. Cuz we have it a lot?
LADY. It's part of doin' business. On any given Friday, year in, year out, you know you can get the world's greatest Salmon Loaf at Lady O'Riley's Pub. What, you want me to go and upset the whole world by serving tuna casserole?
PEG. What if I promise to eat it the next two Fridays in a row? *(Pause.)* Please?
LADY. The tables need setting first. What is it that you like so much about it?
PEG. I like the way it sounds, GE... FILTE... FISH...
LADY. Silly child.
PEG. And I like Mrs. Fleishman... and one day, you're gonna like her too... maybe even be friends...
LADY. Enough. *(To herself.)* Such a dreamer. *(Calling after PEG.)* Take the letter...

(PEG runs through the bar doors into the pub. LADY picks up the letter for ROSE, looks at it, then tosses it back on the counter. Lights fade out on LADY'S kitchen and up on the alley between the two kitchens. PEG comes running around from the front of the pub.)

PEG. I think my grandmother thought I just had a kid's fascination with Mrs. Fleishman, and that when I had discovered all worth discovering in the back room of the deli, I would move on. My grandmother was wrong. The other girls in school... they had a mother and a father, and with that came ballet lessons, and Girl Scouts and family game nights. I, on the

ROSE COLORED GLASS

other hand, had a working grandmother... and a pub... and the freedom to explore, and create whatever world I liked, chores notwithstanding... and I liked a world filled with people and things that were just a little bit different. And I think deep down so did my grandmother, but we were still living in a time where to be different was to be bad. You stuck with the familiar, you hung out with your own... Irish boys drank in Irish pubs. And the world to you... to us... was a world you could reach out and touch. But Mrs. Fleishman was also a lot like my grandmother... she had opinions, and things she believed in... and neither of them was afraid to tell you what they thought...

(Lights fade up on LADY'S kitchen.)

    LADY. All I'm saying is people in this neighborhood are used to doing things a certain way...

(Lights up on ROSE'S kitchen.)

    ROSE. If you can loaf a salmon, I can...
    PEG AND LADY... gefilte' a fish.
    PEG. And that's how they all ended. The rock had met the proverbial hard spot.

(Lights down on LADY'S kitchen, as PEG ENTERS ROSE'S kitchen through the alley door. ROSE is placing a ball of dough into a bowl and covering it with a tea towel.)

    PEG. Hello, Mrs. Fleishman.
    ROSE. I'm gonna start setting my clock by you.
    PEG. Only on Friday.

ROSE COLORED GLASS

ROSE. Salmon Loaf?
PEG. What else? We got one of your letters again.
ROSE. Just leave it on the table.
PEG. I... sorta... forgot it.
ROSE. Then, the next time you come over.
PEG. The letter, it, uh, it looked kinda important.
ROSE. Then run across the alley while I fix you some...
PEG. I would, but I've kinda been in a lot of trouble this week mostly having to do with forgetting things, and, if I have to go back to my grandmother... and tell her I forgot one more thing...
ROSE. Oh, all right...
PEG. I'm afraid she'll get really mad and tell Sister Angeline and then I'll have to go to confession and...
ROSE. All right!

(ROSE takes off her apron, and crosses into the alley. SHE pauses, shrugs, mutters to herself, and looks back at her kitchen.)

ROSE. Oh, for heavens' sake, it is only across the alley...

(ROSE crosses to LADY'S door and knocks.)

ROSE. I believe you have a piece of my mail.
LADY. Not that I choose to.
ROSE. Nor do I. You could put it in my box...
LADY. And I have nothing better to do with my time?
ROSE. I wouldn't know.

(ROSE pauses, not wanting to enter. LADY turns and sees ROSE

ROSE COLORED GLASS

standing outside the door.)

LADY. Oh, all right.

(Without drying her hands, LADY grabs the letter and hands it to ROSE, then returns to her work.)

LADY. *(Under her breath.)* Once in awhile... I could see him making a mistake. But, every time I turn around... *(To ROSE.)* Perhaps you should speak to the postman.

(ROSE turns to her kitchen with the somewhat damp letter.)

ROSE. Perhaps I should. Thank you Mrs. O'Riley.

(ROSE REENTERS her kitchen.)

ROSE. You call a bill from the water department an important piece of mail?
PEG. Maybe the water's just more important in a pub than it is in a deli.
ROSE. Uh-huh. Do you want lunch?
PEG. Can I have what I always have?
ROSE. You like Gefilte fish that much?

(ROSE goes off to get lunch. PEG picks up the letter from Sabina, and begins looking at it.)

PEG. Have you ever thought of having a blue plate special?
ROSE. I think one establishment with that color china is

enough on this block.

(Lights come up on LADY'S kitchen. LADY ENTERS, looks around, goes to the shelves, takes a stack of plates, and begins to head into the bar.)

LADY. Peggy Jean, plates do not walk into the ...

(SHE notices the dish rag on a hook, shakes her head, and grabs it.)

LADY. Nor do tables wash themselves... where is that child?

(LADY EXITS.)

PEG. But say you did have a blue plate special, what would you serve?
ROSE. Salmon Loaf.
PEG. No, really... what would you serve?
ROSE. Salmon Loaf. But not to worry, I'd have it on Tuesdays... on white china.
PEG. That'd be the safest thing. *(ROSE returns with the Gefilte fish.)* ... What are you doing today?
ROSE. Preparing for the Sabbath.

(ROSE takes out her candle sticks and begins to polish them as PEG eats.)

PEG. So, you are working twice as hard today so you can rest up tomorrow?
ROSE. There is a little more to it than just resting.

ROSE COLORED GLASS

PEG. Nanna says it is a little like our Sunday. Know what we do on Sunday? Clean house.
ROSE. That's an odd way to rest.
PEG. Nanna says it's relaxing just to know it's done.
ROSE. Interesting perspective.

(PEG picks up the letter from Sabina.)

PEG. So, how come some of this letter is all blacked out? And how come it took so long to get here?
ROSE. You shouldn't read other people's mail.
PEG. I wasn't reading it... I just noticed the parts that were blacked out. Why is that?
ROSE. There must have been mistakes made.
PEG. A lot of mistakes. Why aren't they crossed out then, or erased?
ROSE. I don't know.
PEG. It just seems odd...
ROSE. *(ROSE goes and grabs the letter from PEG.)* Peg, that's enough.
PEG. I'm sorry I just wanted to know why...
ROSE. And, I don't know why. Now eat your lunch.
PEG. Okay.

(PEG returns to the table, not looking up at ROSE.)

ROSE. *(Feeling a bit guilty.)* Would you like to help me with my strudel?
PEG. I don't know...
ROSE. I could teach you...
PEG. I don't know...

ROSE COLORED GLASS

ROSE. Then you could help me more often...

PEG. Okay...

ROSE. Now, flour your hands and place the dough on the board.

PEG. Right, then we roll and talk. When the church ladies come over to make pies and cinnamon rolls, they talk while they are rolling the dough out. What do you do with your friends?

ROSE. Have you ever thought of just saying what was on your mind?

PEG. *(Pause.)* Do you like Nanna?

ROSE. Do you?

PEG. I asked you first... and I have to, she's my grandmother.

ROSE. No, I believe you have to love people, no one said a thing about having to like anyone...

PEG. I can't imagine you not liking someone. You like me.

ROSE. How could I turn away a five year old shayne maidel with her nose pressed against my window?

PEG. That's true... but how come...

ROSE. It's not as if I dislike your grandmother, we simply disagree on a few things. It goes back a long time. *(Referring to dough.)* Cut the dough into three pieces.

PEG. Right. When you came over with Mr. Fleishman on the boat...

ROSE. We had a cabin on a passenger liner.

PEG. Right. And it was way before I was born... and you had a big Jewish wedding with lots of dancing and you broke a lot of glass.

ROSE. One glass.

PEG. They didn't break anything at Nanna's wedding... it was in Ireland, a whole lot longer ago than your wedding to Mr.

ROSE COLORED GLASS

Fleishman.
ROSE. Peg. Watch the first piece. *(ROSE rolls out the first piece.)*
PEG. You know, I am pretty good at figuring things out. I could help you out with that letter... like I was a spy or something.
ROSE. One thing at a time. Today, you are a baker.
PEG. Right. So, when you got married... I don't think you were very happy because it was re-arranged.
ROSE. Pre-arranged. By a Yenta, a matchmaker. Peg, finish the piece.
PEG. So, you got on a boat and came over here... So, you got to Chicago on a boat?
ROSE. Train. After Baltimore. We heard property was cheap here.
PEG. And you bought the deli. *(SHE takes a wad of dough and places it on the board as the deli.)*... which was right across from the pub. *(SHE places a piece of dough down for the pub, then rips the last piece in two, squeezes them in her hand, and walks them over to the deli as if they were people.)* And, you didn't have any kids right off because you were working so hard in the deli...then all of a sudden he died.

(SHE smashes one of the dough figures.)

ROSE. Not like that! His heart.
PEG. And since you didn't have any kids...
ROSE. He said we should wait, and who was I to question... that anyway.
PEG. If you were Catholic, there would be no questioning at all, you would just start your family right then and there on

your wedding day... but I always figured it was kinda mean of everyone to make them leave their party just to start a family.

ROSE. I think there is more to it than that.

PEG. I sorta wish Nanna had had twins... since she only got one shot at having babies and that being a disappointment to God and all.

ROSE. A disappointment to God?

PEG. When you are Catholic you're supposed to have lots of kids.

ROSE. A concept I never understood.

PEG. Well, really... It's because of my father...

ROSE. And how do you know this?

PEG. Well, one time when the church ladies were over, they were all talking about their children, and Mrs. O'Toole said to Nanna, 'what do you hear from Tommy?' It got really quiet and Nanna said, 'Oh, well, he's traveling a lot, ya' know... Sellin' stuff to the farmers. But we get regular letters. He's doing just fine. Just fine.' When they left, Nanna mumbled something about prying ladies and how she hoped God would forgive her.

ROSE. Oh.

PEG. It's okay. She and Mrs. O'Toole are still friends. *(Pause.)* So, how come you and Nanna never became friends?

ROSE. Can we talk about something else?

PEG. It's the spy in me... so, Mr. Fleishman had died, and then Grandfather died... and you were the only two left, you'd think...

ROSE. Yes, you'd think... but by that time there was a lot of water under the bridge.

PEG. Like what?

ROSE. You should ask your grandmother.

ROSE COLORED GLASS

(Lights up on LADY'S kitchen.)

LADY. This is the last time I am askin' you... don't make me come looking for you.

(Lights fade on LADY'S kitchen.)

PEG. She won't tell me.
ROSE. Sometimes things aren't worth talking about anymore.
PEG. And sometimes it is better... just to come out and say what is on your mind.
ROSE. Look, your grandfather had visions of buying this place for your father.
PEG. The Deli?
ROSE. It was supposed to be a grocery store, a gift so that your father would come home. And when your grandfather couldn't raise the money, and we could, well, he became very bitter. He hated us for everything from stealing his dreams, to invading his neighborhood, to killing Jesus... and if you are hated for everything... then after a while you begin to hate back.
PEG. That was a long time ago, how come you and Nanna...
ROSE. You are brought up to think that your husband is right... for the most part. And when kitchens and bedrooms and workplaces are filled with talk like that...I get a better price on flanken at the meat market, is it because I "Jewed the butcher down" ? Someone slides your grandfather a free beer across the bar, is he "Irish-ing an ale" ? Do you spit on him in the street?
PEG. Did Nanna spit on you in the street?
ROSE. Not in so many words. But if you don't stop an anti-Semitic act, well, it's almost as bad as doing it yourself.

ROSE COLORED GLASS

PEG. What is that?

(While all this is happening, LADY steps out into the alley, looks around, then walks over to ROSE'S kitchen, and looks in. SHE sees ROSE working with PEG, takes a deep breath, and walks back toward the alley.)

LADY. PEGGY JEAN... I am not settin' your tables for you... and we eat off of plates on a BLUE PLATE Friday. Now move!
ROSE. Ask your Grandmother.
PEG. Coming! I was just...
LADY. PEGGY JEAN, DON'T MAKE ME COME OVER THERE.
ROSE. Go.

(PEG EXITS to the alley to an awaiting LADY.)

PEG. I was just helping Mrs. Fleishman with her...
LADY. I know exactly what you were doing. Both of you.

(LADY turns back to her kitchen, followed by PEG. Lights fade on ROSE'S kitchen, and up on the alley as PEG crosses into it.)

PEG. It just didn't seem right that husbands who had been dead for a very long time should go on hurting the women they loved. And now was as good a time as any to fix that. Father Patrick had said we should love our neighbor... somehow.

(PEG goes to LADY'S mail box, and finds it empty. SHE goes

ROSE COLORED GLASS

to ROSE'S box, opens it, sorts through the mail, takes a letter out and goes into LADY'S kitchen. LADY is making bread.)

PEG. Mail's here. There's never anything for me.

LADY. One day... one day.

PEG. You know, you could write to me in care of Mrs. Fleishman's. Then I'd get mail.

LADY. And how would that look? *(Pause. Then PEG starts back out to the alley.)* Not for another week. You promised me two blue plate Fridays.

PEG. If I ordered something from the mail order catalogue, I'd get mail.

LADY. Not very personal.

PEG. It would be if I ordered something from the lingerie department.

LADY. Since when did you become interested in lingerie?

PEG. Nanna...

LADY. And, besides, Roberts Department Store has a nice... respectable selection.

PEG. But, it would be more exciting to get it in the mail.

LADY. I suppose so, if you don't mind it being too small. You can buy the exact same dress at Roberts... but order it through the mail, and it's two sizes too small. I don't know if it's the mail itself, or that they know that most people won't bother to send it back...

PEG. I'll order it two sizes too big.

LADY. And look like Aunt Nell? How many floral patterned potato sacks can one own in a lifetime.

PEG. But, I betcha underneath she's wearing mail order lingerie.

ROSE COLORED GLASS

LADY. I highly doubt it...

PEG. Look, you got one with funny stamps on it... oh, it's not for us.

LADY. And why does this not surprise me... Vienna.

PEG. That's in Austria.

LADY. I know where Vienna is. Run it over to her.

PEG. The stamps are different than before...

(LADY turns the envelope and looks at the stamp.)

LADY. Adolf... Hitler...

PEG. Isn't he the new king of Austria?

LADY. Hardly child. Odd though... it's on a letter from Vienna... run it over to her.

PEG. I'll just tell her it's here.

LADY. Just take it over

PEG. Wouldn't it be nicer... friendlier... if Mrs. Fleishman just came over and got it...

LADY. It would be nicer if you just did what I asked... for once.

PEG. But say she did... just drop in...you would be polite and courteous wouldn't you?

LADY. I am always polite.

PEG. Not when Eddie Courtney comes by...

LADY. Eddie Courtney is the town drunk, looking for a hand-out, and she is Mrs. Fleishman... I'm sure there must be a difference.

PEG. Meaning if she came over you would be polite.

LADY. Yes, child, I would be polite.

PEG. Promise?

LADY. Yes. I promise... now run the letter over.

ROSE COLORED GLASS

PEG. I can't. It's illegal to redeliver mail... especially from a foreign country.

(PEG runs out the back and into the alley.)

PEG. Two weeks had passed since I swore they would be friends and this was the first real window of opportunity I had, and anyway, how hard could it be to bring two worlds only an alley apart, together? So, I grabbed the rock of opportunity and threw it at the hardest spot I could find... my grandmother. She had promised to be polite. It was a start.

(PEG runs over to ROSE'S kitchen and knocks on the door. PEG returns to LADY'S kitchen and sits on stool, staring out the window.)

LADY. And, what is it that's goin' on in that mind of yours? Starin' off into space...
PEG. Why don't you like her?
LADY. Who is it I'm not likin'?
PEG. Mrs. Fleishman.
LADY. It is very complicated.
PEG. Mrs. Fleishman says there's a lot of water under the bridge.
LADY. For once, perhaps she is right.
PEG. So, why can't you just walk across the bridge, without looking down, then you won't see all the water and you can...
LADY. It is just not that easy.
PEG. Have you ever Jewed the butcher down?
LADY. WHAT? Where did you hear that?

ROSE COLORED GLASS

PEG. I... ah... Mrs. Fleishman was talking about anti semi... something...

LADY. Is that what she's serving up now with her Gelfilte fish?

PEG. No, no... I don't even know for sure...what that means.

LADY. And that's the way it's going to stay.

PEG. I'm sorry, Nanna... You could make it easier... we could make it easier... just by being nice... maybe... that anti-stuff... could go away... by being nice, and all... oh, look, Mrs. Fleishman...

(ROSE knocks lightly on screen door and PEG ushers her in.)

ROSE. I understand you got a piece of my mail by mistake...

LADY. Yes?

PEG. Please, Nanna...

LADY. Yes, Mrs. Fleishman... I could have run it across the alley.

ROSE. *(Under her breath.)* That would be the day.

LADY. Excuse me?

ROSE. It is just as easy for me to run across the alley as...

LADY. It's on the counter... my hands are full of flour.

PEG. We get a lot of mail, and sometimes the postman...

LADY. Can't tell a good Irish Pub from a Jewish Delicatessen.

(ROSE stands looking at the mail.)

LADY. *(Cont'd.)* It is, after all, a government job. There ought to be some sort of standards...

ROSE COLORED GLASS

(PEG hands ROSE the letter.)

PEG. The stamp is from Austria. You could open it here. We hardly ever get mail from far away.

(ROSE runs her thumb over the stamp of Hitler.)

LADY. *(Notices ROSE.)* Is there something else I can get for you, Mrs. Fleishman?
PEG. Nanna.
ROSE. I got what I came for.
PEG. Mrs. Fleishman... Grandmother! You promised!

(ROSE begins to EXIT.)

LADY. Yes. I promised to be courteous... watching someone reading mail was not part of the bargain.
ROSE. She is right. Good day.
PEG. Nanna... Mrs. Fleishman... you could stay and have tea. It would be the courteous thing to do...
LADY. Peg...
PEG. And, maybe there would be something interesting in the letter to talk about... over tea... in that courteous sort of way. And I could make the tea. Mrs. Fleishman, how would you like your tea? With sugar or lemon? Nanna takes her's with a little sugar, and sometimes at night with a shot of...
LADY. Oh, all right, Peg. Mrs. Fleishman, stay for tea and read your mail.
ROSE. Thank you, anyway.

ROSE COLORED GLASS

(PEG looks at LADY as if to remind her of her promise.)

 LADY. No, really... I have tea...
 ROSE. I really don't think I should... bread day is not a good day for breaking new ground.
 LADY. I know this child too well, Mrs. Fleishman... She will not let up until you read your mail and I am... well... please, stay for tea.
 ROSE. If you're sure it is not too much trouble.

(LADY stays frozen for a second, then turns toward the tea.)

 ROSE. Letters from Europe are as often bad as they are good... sometimes it is good to have someone with you when...
 LADY. Perhaps you'd rather wait, and read it with your friends... I know that when I have bad news... I go running to the women at the church...
 ROSE. Yes. But we are not like that... close-knit...
 LADY. *(PEG stares at LADY.)* Then, stay. At least have tea...
 ROSE. I really don't think this is such a good idea.
 PEG. No, it will be fine. Here, sit right here.
 LADY. *(To PEG.)* Don't you have tables to set?
 PEG. I finished the tables.

(ROSE has opened the letter and is looking at it intently.)

 LADY. Then go play with a friend.
 PEG. I don't have any friends. I have you and Mrs. Fleishman.
 LADY. Then, I suggest you find some...

ROSE COLORED GLASS

PEG. Just stand out in the street and hail one down, like a cab, or something?
ROSE. Find something to do, child.

(PEG looks to LADY, who nods and motions her outside. PEG EXITS into the alley.)

PEG. I had never been told by Mrs. Fleishman to find something to do. Nor had she ever called me child. I had always thought of us as equals... as much as a grown-up and a kid, who still has to call her Mrs. Fleishman, can be. *(Pause.)* So, I hung out in the alley, and kicked rocks. First one at the deli, then the pub, and back and forth. When neither one of them wants you around, it's hardly a time to take sides.

(Lights fade on alley as PEG kicks rocks.)

LADY. Sugar?
ROSE. Bitte.
LADY. *(Not understanding.)* Mrs. Fleishman...

(ROSE finally looks up from the letter. PEG moves over to the door to eavesdrop.)

ROSE. Please.
LADY. *(SHE serves her tea.)* Is everything all right?
ROSE. Yes. I'm sure it will be. *(Taking the tea.)* This is very nice. Thank you.

(ROSE folds the letter and puts it back in its envelope. As SHE does, a piece of a photograph falls onto the floor.)

ROSE COLORED GLASS

LADY. Oh, here. Something fell from the... *(SHE picks it up and looks at it.)* A piece of photograph.

(ROSE extends her hand, as LADY unconsciously puts on her glasses for a closer look.)

LADY. *(Cont'd.)* It looks like a young boy...

(SHE hands it to ROSE, who stares at it.)

ROSE. My god... kinehora...
LADY. Mrs. Fleishman?

(ROSE gathers up the letter.)

LADY. *(Cont'd.)* Where are you going?
ROSE. Back to work.

(SHE EXITS into the alley and stays there.)

LADY. *(Stepping into the alley.)* Mrs. Fleishman, what is the matter?
ROSE. Nothing. Everything is all right, I must get...
LADY. Everything is not all right.
ROSE. It is nothing.
LADY. Mrs. Fleishman, that photograph has obviously...
ROSE. Oh, all right. His name is Abraham. He is my sister's son. I have not seen a photograph of him in a long while. And now... this.
LADY. Mrs. Fleishman... I don't make tea just to have it

ROSE COLORED GLASS

thrown down the drain...waste not, want not.
ROSE. What?
LADY. Nothing. *(Eyeing PEG in the alley.)* Come in for that tea...someone would say it was rude of me to... Mrs. Fleishman?
ROSE. Fine.

(LADY opens the door and escorts ROSE in. PEG pops up, as if to join them and is stopped by LADY.)

LADY. Friends....
PEG. I'm workin' on it!

(ROSE and LADY sit on the stools, and for a second sip tea. PEG listens at the door, hears the silence, then in frustration, goes to ROSE'S mailbox, slams down the lid. BOTH hear it.)

LADY. So...the letter... it came with a picture...
ROSE. Yes. Abraham. My sister could have left Austria when visas were easy to get. I should have insisted.

(Again PEG slams the mail box.)

ROSE. All right, Peg.

(ROSE turns to the letter. SHE takes it out and reads.)

ROSE. Here. Meine Liebe Rose, I fear this is the last time I will be able to write. It is getting harder and harder to move about freely... money is scarce... your old friend Victor has been sent... *(Showing LADY.)* It has been marked out... *(Reading.)* The visas we applied for last spring are being held, so plans for the holiday are uncertain. Local youth seem to find even the smallest adventure out of a simple trip to the countryside. We should all see life through rose colored glass... And I love that. Now, don't forget that.

LADY. It is such an odd letter...

ROSE. Even for my sister.

LADY. But, why?

ROSE. This is the first mention of any long planned holiday, and the closest Abraham will ever get to a trip to the great outdoors is a concert in the park.

LADY. Perhaps a new friend?

ROSE. He is 11. I am sure by now my sister has convinced him that the parks of Vienna contain all the flora and fauna he will ever need to see.

LADY. Then why the talk of holidays and colored glass?

ROSE. When my sister was young she had ways of getting what she wanted without just coming out and saying it. She would say to you "this piece by Strauss is the most beautiful I have ever heard... now don't forget that". And there would appear in some shop window that small gold music box that played Strauss. And because Papa loved her so much, it soon became hers.

LADY. Then where are you to look for rose colored glass?

ROSE. I have no idea. Papa can no longer send me down to Van Meir's to ask what he has in a Strauss melody this season. She was mine to take care of then... but what can I do now?

(PEG moves to the alley door to eavesdrop. The women are still for a moment, an awkward silence.)

ROSE COLORED GLASS

LADY. I am sorry about the letter...
ROSE. My sister's holiday plans are really nothing to be sorry about.
LADY. It's obviously more...
ROSE. Is it? *(Pause.)* Well, let us hope you are wrong, Mrs. O'Riley.
LADY. Yes. Let us.

(ROSE EXITS to her kitchen and puts the photo in the music box on her table.)

PEG. Perhaps in the act of trying to be polite... my grandmother had become curious about a letter... and in a small way about the woman across the alley.

(LADY steps out into the alley to shake out a tea towel, as ROSE steps out to look in her mailbox, takes out a letter that has been returned to her as undeliverable. The women see each other.)

LADY. Good morning, Mrs. Fleishman...
ROSE. Mrs. O'Riley

(ROSE and LADY return to their kitchens.)

PEG. And they began to acknowledge each other in the alley. It was a start...
LADY. It was an isolated incident.
PEG. It was an isolated incident. That's what the newspapers said. But, Mrs. Fleishman said it was an excuse for putting

your head in the sand... She made me read the papers too. By the end of August, 1938, reports of "isolated incidences" of German brutality toward the Jews began to be found on the back pages of the big newspapers. We read reports of Jewish communities being herded into ghettos, like cattle, of forced labor, of random executions right there in the streets... yet all, isolated...

(Lights fade up on ROSE in the alley. LADY is working on her ledger.)

ROSE.... Isolated incidences... How can you look at the imprisonment of 2,000 Jewish professors as an isolated incident?
LADY. *(To ROSE in alley.)* You don't know that as a fact.
ROSE. How many does it take? 2,000? 5,000?
LADY. I understand you're worried about your family...
ROSE. That is the one isolated incident I can put names to.
LADY. ... but shouting in the ally is not going to change anything. *(To herself.)* Lord, you put a pot of tea on for the woman, next thing ya' know she's screaming at you whenever she takes a fancy.

(LADY closes her books and goes to her door, and looks out.)

ROSE. How many do they have to shoot down in the street before...
LADY. Mrs. Fleishman, what is going on out here?
ROSE. *(Pause.)* I have come to borrow sugar.
LADY. Sugar? You want to borrow sugar?
ROSE. Fine. I'll make it with lemon.

ROSE COLORED GLASS

(ROSE begins to go back into her kitchen.)

LADY. Mrs. Fleish... Rose. What... what is it you want?
ROSE. Sugar... all right, I should have never opened that letter over here. I should have opened it in front of my stock boy. My stock boy has to listen to me... I pay him.
LADY. Maybe you should talk to someone at your synagogue.
ROSE. I can't...

(LADY stares at ROSE.)

LADY. Why not?
ROSE. We all have somebody missing...
LADY. I don't understand... you've never borrowed anything before and now...
ROSE. Fine. I won't take the sugar.

(ROSE opens her kitchen door to go in.)

LADY. Stop! *(Pause.)* How much... sugar, do you need? A cup?
ROSE. A teaspoon.
LADY. A teaspoon?
ROSE. And a half.
LADY. A teaspoon and a half... Rose, no one in their right mind walks across the alley for a teaspoon and a... I am sorry... Perhaps, you would like to have that tea over here...
ROSE. You do have sugar?
LADY. Yes! Come, we will have tea... and sugar... and if

ROSE COLORED GLASS

we must, we will talk...

(ROSE and LADY ENTER LADY'S kitchen..)

> ROSE. Thank you... I don't even know where to start.
> LADY. It's not as if we've had a whole lot of practice.

(LADY motions for her to sit. ROSE looks around, and sits on the stool.)

> ROSE. Some of us... many of us, are having letters returned from Europe stamped "unable to deliver"... we are hearing nothing. Nothing but terrifying rumors and what little is printed in the newspaper. We are not even certain what...
> LADY. Rose... Europe, it is so far away... it is not our problem. We have trouble enough here taking care of our own...
> ROSE. My sister is one of our OWN. When you begin to take away her possessions, her livelihood, her home, her dignity... then it ought to become our problem.
> LADY. What is it you want from me?
> ROSE. I need to find them. People just don't disappear off the face of the earth.
> LADY. Then start at the top and work down.
> ROSE. This is America... is that God or Mr. Roosevelt?
> LADY. Eleanor.

(ROSE smiles.)

> ROSE. I shall remember that.
> LADY. What?
> ROSE. You made me smile at a difficult time.

ROSE COLORED GLASS

LADY. I... the top. There's an agency or committee, or sub-committee in this country for everything else, surely...
ROSE. The phone book. *(Calling for PEG.)* Peg, run over to Rabbi Schulman's and ask to borrow his Washington, DC phone book...
PEG. But I'm not...
ROSE. Tell him it's for Rose Fleishman. Run.

(PEG runs into the alley, as ROSE goes into her kitchen. Lights fade on LADY'S kitchen, and up on alley.)

PEG. That's right. They both gave permission for a good Irish "Catholic" girl to go running like crazy through the middle of a synagogue, right to the Rabbi's office and ask to... borrow a phone book. It was beautiful... it was a dare. That is, until I got there. Not being privy to the details, and all, I told him it had something to do with Europe, and she had to talk to the President's wife. The phone book he said was for later, he would see that she got it in synagogue... for now he handed me a contraption he called a...

(Lights fade on alley and up on LADY'S kitchen as ROSE ENTERS with a radio, followed by PEG.)

ROSE. ... a short wave radio.
LADY. What?
ROSE. A short wave... I want to listen to the news in Europe.
PEG. Rabbi Schulman gave it to us... her.
LADY. That's an awful lot of trouble to go to just to hear the news.

ROSE COLORED GLASS

ROSE. They're not reporting all of it over here.
LADY. That's ridiculous.
ROSE. Over here... if you ignore it, maybe it'll go away.
LADY. What'll go away?
ROSE. I'm not sure... but I plan to find out.
LADY. I thought you sent her after a phone book.
ROSE. I did.
LADY. And he sends her back with this?
ROSE. He knows what he is doing... where is your faith, Mrs. O'Riley?
LADY. Right where it belongs. Father Patrick would never send one home with something like this...
ROSE. Then Father Patrick should start listening to...
LADY. To who?
ROSE. Will you help me make this thing work?
LADY. To who?
ROSE. Please?
PEG. I know who.
LADY. Homework. Do your homework. *(Pause.)* Why not your kitchen?
ROSE. It's Jewish...
LADY. So?
ROSE. And yours is Irish...

(ROSE begins to tune the radio.)

LADY. And what? You expect the Nazis to catch you spying?
ROSE. Aren't we witty today? If I remember right, your Mr. O'Riley, rest in peace, was quite handy with gadgets. I was hoping some of it had rubbed off and you could help me.

ROSE COLORED GLASS

LADY. Ah, my Paddy had a way with the mechanical... could take things apart, AND put them back together just the way they were.

PEG. That would explain the big jar of extra nuts and bolts we have...

LADY. Unnecessary parts.

ROSE. Can you help me here?

(ROSE begins to fuss with the knobs. LADY smacks the top of the radio with her hand, which produces static.)

LADY. That's about all he ever taught me...

ROSE. Then I came to the right spot. *(SHE again adjusts the dial.)* Shhh.

VOICE OVER. *(Static.)*... to the BBC... it's 10 PM. At the top of the news this evening...

PEG. We got something.

VOICE OVER. Hitler's forces continue to sweep over Eastern Europe towards Czechoslovakia. Great Britain has assured France of Britain's support should they become involved in the war. British Prime Minister Chamberlain said, "How incredible it is that we should be digging trenches and laying in gas masks here because of a quarrel in..." *(Static.)*

ROSE. Don't fade out on me now...

LADY. What is it you expect to hear, exactly?

ROSE. I don't know... some truth...

VOICE OVER. It was announced today that the Intergovernmental Committee has been meeting in London since August. The Committee is the only solid result of the Conference at Evian. *(Static.)*

ROSE. Damn...

ROSE COLORED GLASS

(SHE again fusses with the radio.)

PEG. What's Evian?

ROSE. It was a conference of world leaders. They gathered together to talk about the European refugee problem. So many people are being forced out of their countries... and are looking for a place to live... anywhere. But the countries, one by one, they all stood up and found reasons to not take the refugees. They did not want to even consider being part of the solution. Australia, koala, kangaroos, they jumped up and said, "We do not have a racial problem, and we do not want one!" That is what Evian was. Fah Shtaste?

LADY. How do you know all this?

ROSE. Back pages of the paper... *(Static begins to clear.)* Wait...

VOICE OVER. And tonight we again bring you words of wisdom, thought provoking ideas from around the world. The cow jumped over the moon and has landed on a star.

PEG. What does that mean?

ROSE. They are messages to family members far away... Rabbi Schulman says they repeat a whole series of them every night.

PEG. But how will they know if the right person gets it? I just don't understand how anyone could think that a silly message like that would get to the right person... all the way over here in... Chicago, or Detroit, or someplace...

ROSE. Now, Peg O'Riley, where is that faith of yours? If you don't try something... as silly as it may seem to others... you will never know if it could work...

PEG. But...

ROSE COLORED GLASS

ROSE. But nothing. Have a little faith, child.
LADY. You really believe it will work?
ROSE. Until I see differently, yes.
LADY. That's a whole lot of hogwash... and so is this.
ROSE. Shhhh.

(Lights shift. They all stand listening, then EXIT one by one. Shortwave stays lit and we hear:)

VOICE OVER. Purple tulips are now in season and finally available for export. Samuel was here, took his bride, and moved to the land of sand.

(Short wave montage, voice-overs intercut with news, music and the women's actions moving on and off stage. Lights change. Time passes. The shortwave stays lit.)

VOICE OVER. German-Austrian Stormtroopers continue to terrorize Central Europe as 51 Austrian Jews including an 81-year-old Rabbi were left to starve to death on a stone breakwater in the middle of the Danube where Austria, Czechoslovakia, and Hungry meet. Picked up by Czech patrol boats, they were fed and clothed. However, fearing this would accelerate the recent wave of Nazi violence against the Jews, the Czech government loaded them on to trucks that took them back across the border, where Hungarian Border Patrols picked them up and deposited them back in Austria. The 51 Jews were then arrested by the Nazis for illegal entry.

(PEG ENTERS to get plates, turns radio up loud, EXITS.)

ROSE COLORED GLASS

VOICE OVER. Tonight we again bring you words of wisdom, thought provoking ideas from around the world. Local youth seem to find even the smallest adventure out of a simple trip to the countryside.

(The women come running back into LADY'S kitchen.)

VOICE OVER. *(Cont'd.)* They seem to see things through rose colored glass...
PEG. That's what...
ROSE. Shh.
VOICE OVER. *(Cont'd.)* Even in this heavy fog... You're listening this evening...

(ROSE snaps off the radio.)

LADY. Rose?
ROSE. Gut in himmel. My sister... they must be all right. She found a way to get her message to me.
PEG. It worked! It really worked!
LADY. I think you're really stretching this.
PEG. In code and everything!
ROSE. She told me what never to forget, and the BBC just told me where to look for it.
LADY. What fog then? Whose fog?
ROSE. Their fog... I don't know... London's fog. *(A thought.)* The Quakers! I have heard that the Quakers will help the refugees get messages to their families. *(To PEG.)* I need the phone book from Rabbi Schulman, now, and tell him we have found my family.
PEG. We have?

ROSE COLORED GLASS

ROSE. They're somewhere in England. I wonder how many times they have already broadcast my message?
LADY. You seem awfully sure about this.
ROSE. I have to be.
LADY. Rose, he said it's only youth who see things through rose colored glass.
ROSE. Surely the family must be together...
LADY. Yes.

(Lights fade on LADY'S kitchen and up on the alley. PEG ENTER the alley.)

PEG. So, again, I ran through the synagogue. Rabbi Schulman insisted on delivering the phone book himself... the short wave radio he would let me have... but not the phone book. I figure at one point he must have had a bad experience with a good Irish girl, and a phone book...

(Lights fade on alley as PEG runs off. Lights up on ROSE at the table writing. It is late. PEG stands in the alley. ROSE gets up to stretch and walks out into the alley. SHE is a bit surprised to find PEG out there.)

ROSE. Isn't it past your bedtime?
PEG. I'm not sure.
ROSE. You're not sure?
PEG. When I came to live here, we never really established a set time.
ROSE. Really?
PEG. But over the years, I've found 9:30 sorta makes everyone happy.

ROSE COLORED GLASS

(There is a long pause as PEG fiddles with a card.)

ROSE. Mail?
PEG. Not really. It's a card from my Dad.
ROSE. That's nice...
PEG. A birthday card. Four months and three days late. From Iowa. And I know how to read a postmark... so I know it doesn't take that long.
ROSE. Your father lives in Iowa?
PEG. He lives all over. Nanna says he's running.
ROSE. Running?
PEG. Running away. From the memory of Momma... from everything. Maybe from Nanna. Maybe from me.
ROSE. He most likely is running away from himself...
PEG. I didn't make Momma die. I was only 4 1/2. We could have stayed together in California or Iowa or wherever. Been a family. Just the two of us... But Nanna told him to come home.
ROSE. And he did.
PEG. Just long enough to drop me off.
ROSE. Perhaps he thought you would be happier with your Grandmother.
PEG. Maybe... but I betcha I'll never see him again.
ROSE. It's all right to miss him...
PEG. At least you and Nanna know what you are missing.
ROSE. Your father is an adult. When he gets things figured out, he'll be back. And, then again, maybe he won't be. But, dwelling on it won't...
PEG. I'm not dwelling...
ROSE. Try not to think about it. Just because you want somebody to do something, doesn't mean they are going to do

ROSE COLORED GLASS

it... You want to come in? *(Pause.)* I have strudel... cherry strudel... a big piece.
    PEG. Okay.

(ROSE and PEG go inside.)

    PEG. *(Looking at the paperwork on the table.)* What is this stuff?
    ROSE. The results of your latest mad dash through the synagogue.
    PEG. I went to the Rabbi's outside door!
    ROSE. Uh, huh.
    PEG. Why don't people like the Jews?
    ROSE. People hate each other.
    PEG. Why?
    ROSE. Human nature.
    PEG. Do you miss your sister?
    ROSE. Read me the next one on the list, please.
    PEG. You got all these from the phone book? The department of Human and Social Services, 331 17th Street, Northwest.
    ROSE. Is that in Washington?
    PEG. Yes. So, how many of these have you done?
    ROSE. A little over a dozen.
    PEG. What are you writing them about?
    ROSE. I tell them that I am looking for a little boy...
    PEG. And what about his parents?
    ROSE. *(Pointedly.)* I tell them that I am looking for an 11-year-old boy named Abraham Sachs who is living somewhere in England, and hopefully they can put me in contact with someone, or some agency that can help me find him.

ROSE COLORED GLASS

PEG. Are you going to send the picture?

ROSE. Fa macht da moil. I couldn't part with it. *(Touching the music box.)* I simply tell them that he looks very much like his mother... he has her eyes.

PEG. And his ears. What about his ears?

ROSE. I have never thought about Abraham in terms of ears.

PEG. Too bad. Cuz if he looked anything like my cousin Francis, you could just call the King and tell him to look for a red head with ears that look like tubas...

ROSE. Peg.

PEG. Oh, sorry. But, he'd be the first to point that out...

ROSE. Peg. The next name on the list?

PEG. Oh. The American... I'm sorry I made fun of my cousin, Mrs. Fleishman. I know it's not a nice thing to do.

ROSE. That's true... and it's a little hard for me to understand, we don't have any ear problems in our family.

PEG. Lucky you... What sort of problems do you have?

ROSE. Peg.

PEG. Sorry. The American Jewish Joint Distribution Committee, 7711 South...

LADY. *(ENTERING the alley and calling.)* Peg. Peg O'Riley. It's 9:32.

PEG. Oh, I gotta go.

ROSE. Thank you for your help...

PEG. Sure.

LADY. PEG!

PEG. Coming!

ROSE. Good night, Peg.

PEG. See ya'... ah, good night, Mrs. Fleishman.

ROSE COLORED GLASS

(PEG kisses ROSE good night, and EXITS into the alley. SHE shows the card to LADY, who reads it.)

LADY. Some people face life by running away. Others by looking it square in the face.
PEG. He doesn't come home because he can't look at my face.
LADY. What?
PEG. I was five. I remember, Nanna. He said he couldn't sit at the breakfast table and look into Momma's eyes... do you think I have Momma's eyes?
LADY. Yes. And they are very pretty.

(LADY hugs PEG and then sends her into LADY'S kitchen.)

LADY. Oh, Tommy! *(Looking at the card.)* Why does God keep punishing me for letting you go? Iowa! It's not my fault you had wanderin' feet like your father. It's not my fault Paddy couldn't hear ya' when ya' tried to tell him so...

(LADY moves into her kitchen, grabs a bottle of whiskey off the shelf, pours a shot, drinks it, and holds the letter.)

LADY. Tommy, I got a pub to run and I'm pourin' beer and feeding everyone in the neighborhood as fast as I can, and every time I turn around Father Patrick's asking me to serve at the soup kitchen, and then the Catholic ladies are always wanting cookies for another one of their bazaars... And now I got the poor Jewish lady borrowing sugar and screamin' about Europe... and, on top of all of that, I have your 13-year-old daughter... I let you go because you said it was killin' you to stay. Well, it killed Paddy when you left. God, I'm an old woman. When is enough enough???

(LADY takes the bottle and letter and EXITS into the pub. Lights fade up on alley as PEG ENTERS.)

PEG. And the fall evenings passed, one after another, with the lights burning in her kitchen till the wee hours of the night. And I tried not to think about it. And for the most part it worked. Thanksgiving was coming up soon, and I spent one day trying to figure out what she was going to have on that day, being Jewish and all. She said she was American and would have turkey like everyone else... only with a matzoh dressing. I think she added the matzoh dressing part to make me feel really stupid for asking. But I don't think Mrs. Fleishman was thinking much about the holiday... On November 11, Rabbi Schulman came by with a copy of the Chicago Daily Tribune... *(PEG picks up the paper.)* and the headline read "Nazis Smash, Loot and Burn Jewish Shops and Temples Until Goebbels Calls Halt". The Nazis went on a rampage and burned almost 200 synagogues, more than 800 shops destroyed, and another 7,500 looted. The streets of Germany and Austria were littered by the shattered shop windows and the disaster became know as Kristallnacht... night of the broken glass... 20,000 Jews were arrested and taken to concentration camps... On top of it all the Jews were fined 4 billion marks for the destruction... a world a whole ocean away was beginning to explode. The mistake was we thought it was too far away for us to hear.

(Lights fade on alley as LADY crosses to ROSE'S kitchen.)

ROSE COLORED GLASS

LADY. *(ENTERING.)* So, how do you gefilte-a-fish?
ROSE. And good evening to you. The same way you loaf-a-salmon. Only we boil it.
LADY. Lovely.
ROSE. Actually, it is...Why are you here?
LADY. Oh, I've caught you at a bad time. I'll just...
ROSE. Would you like a cup of coffee?
LADY. If it's not too much...
ROSE. It's not... it's made already. *(Long pause.)* So, that's how you start off a visit... with idle conversation about fish?
LADY. Would you prefer I scream across the alley about politics, then ask to borrow sugar?
ROSE. At least I'd know what was on your mind.

(LADY notices the large stack of letters on the table.)

LADY. How are things going?

(ROSE moves to the letters, and picks up some of them.)

ROSE. I'd have more success with a blue plate special... even on Tuesday. Here. *(SHE pulls out letters from a stack.)* Hebrew Sheltering and Immigration Aid Society... would love to help, especially with funding... once we have located the child. The Council on Human Rights... requires a visa/passport number before they can even begin... The Department of Social Services... out of their range of activities... it is not our department... *(Tossing letters.)* Not our department. Not our department... NOT OUR PROBLEM. Oh, here's a good one... Section 7-C of the Immigration Act of 1924 requires the following public records: two copies of the birth certificate, a record of military service and a police certificate of good character for the previous five years... from his country of origin.

LADY. But he's only 11.

ROSE. He's had a birthday.

LADY. Surely there must be an exception...

ROSE. But till then...

LADY. ... you're nowhere.

ROSE. Yes. I'm only looking for a needle in a haystack.

LADY. *(Pause.)* Rose... On Thursday afternoon... I was in church, and I was speaking to a few ladies about your situation...

ROSE. My situation?

LADY. With the boy...

ROSE. It is now the subject of idle conversation... of useless prayer circles.

LADY. How dare you? They are anything but useless. Every Thursday afternoon a group of fine Catholic ladies gather in the basement of St. Mary's church for a small program of events and talk, and sharin' what's goin' on with each other and we start and end with a prayer and what the hell, we were just trying to help... that's all...

ROSE. I don't need that kind of help.

LADY. What could it hurt?

ROSE. Words of pity or sympathy... oh, the poor Jew across the alley from Mrs. O'Riley...

LADY. Why does it always come back to that?

ROSE. You're not the one scraping "Jew Go Home" off your shop windows.

LADY. Well, the ladies in church aren't responsible for that dirt and if that's all you think we're capable of... words of pity. Fine. Then fight this battle of yours on your own, Mrs.

ROSE COLORED GLASS

Fleishman... I shan't say another word.

(SHE EXITS through the door to the alley.)

    ROSE. That will be the day.

(PEG has been standing in the alley, eavesdropping.)

    LADY. What are you doing up?

(ROSE puts her head down on the table.)

    ROSE. Sheisse.
    LADY. I heard that.
    PEG. Me too.
    ROSE. Fine. Then it shall make wonderful gossip for next Thursday afternoon...

(LADY reaches in her pocket, and finds a scrap of paper, looks at it, and puts it back in her pocket.)

    PEG. You're not going to give it to her?
    LADY. You heard her, she doesn't need my help.

(LADY goes into her kitchen and hangs her apron on the back of the door.)

    LADY. Peggy Jean, off to bed.
    PEG. I'm, ah, just gonna get a drink of water.
    LADY. All right. But I expect the lights off in here in five minutes... and I've counted the cinnamon rolls so don't get any

bright ideas.

(LADY goes off into the pub, PEG sees the apron, looks through the bar doors, then grabs the note from the apron pocket, and runs out into the alley.)

PEG. And, that's exactly what I needed... a bright idea... for without one I was just a common thief...

(PEG looks at the piece of paper, as we hear LADY heading back.)

LADY. PEGGY JEAN O'RILEY... .

(PEG is startled by LADY and drops the piece of paper. SHE looks at it for a split second, smiles, and begins banging on ROSE'S door.)

PEG. Mrs. Fleishman... Mrs. Fleishman...

(PEG runs to LADY'S kitchen, and yells inside.)

PEG. Nanna... come quickly.

(Both women arrive at their doors at the same time.)

ROSE. What is it, child?
LADY. Peggy Jean, what is going on... oh.
ROSE. Oh.

(PEG runs to the piece of paper, picks it up.)

ROSE COLORED GLASS

PEG. I found the piece of paper out here in the alley, with that important number on it. Nanna, you must have dropped it on the way in... or... *(Turning to ROSE with a new idea.)* maybe it was slid in the side of your door, and the wind caught it, and blew it into the alley... and, it's a good thing I found it, what with the street cleaners and all...

LADY. Street cleaners, that I would like to see...

ROSE. Just give me the note.

PEG. Maybe Nanna better... her handwriting is not as good as it used to be... it looks like the number for Herman Lewis's chicken aid...

LADY. German Jewish Children's Aid... for heavens sake...

PEG. Well, if the letters are that bad... then the numbers could be really... bad

LADY. Just give her the note, she can figure it out herself.

PEG. But what if she got it just one number off... she could be ringing Louisa's Pizzeria... that would be very embarrassing... and Nanna you couldn't blame Mrs. Fleishman if she said, "How odd, I got this number from my friend, Lady O'Riley"... and then it could get back to you... and that wouldn't look good... maybe you should go into the deli... and let her write it down for herself...

LADY. And, who says she even wants it...

PEG. *(To ROSE.)* It just might come in handy. *(To LADY.)* And it would make you feel better. Nanna please, it's getting past my bed time...

LADY. All right... all right. But go to bed. Go, I don't do humbling in front of a crowd... Go.

PEG. Okay...

LADY. Go!

ROSE COLORED GLASS

(PEG EXITS into LADY'S kitchen. LADY and ROSE pause in the alley. They look at each other, then LADY hands the paper to ROSE.)

LADY. Here. It's the address of the German Jewish Children's Aid. They have an office in London. We thought it might help.

(ROSE takes the paper from LADY and goes into the Deli kitchen, and turns to LADY.)

ROSE. What is this number... a four?

(LADY takes the paper, and looks at it closely.)

LADY. Ah, no... a nine.

(LADY moves to leave, then turns back.)

ROSE. I can figure the rest of this out myself.
LADY. You don't have to do this by yourself...
ROSE. It's my family.
LADY. Fine. Then you get on that white horse of yours with all the pride and stubbornness you can muster... and go riding off into...
ROSE. Into what?
LADY. I don't know... I just hope that you can do this... before you are worried about not just finding him... but finding him alive. Why can't you just shove some of that damn pride of yours in a drawer someplace, and think about the boy...

ROSE COLORED GLASS

ROSE. This is what you call humbling?
LADY. I didn't say who was going to be humbled.
ROSE. True. *(Pause.)* What? I should thank you?
LADY. Fine. Be that way.

(SHE begins to EXIT.)

ROSE. Wait. *(Pause.)* I'm... sorry.
LADY. Is that so?
ROSE. You are very good at this humbling business... and, you are right.
LADY. About what?
ROSE. Everything... absolutely everything. For heaven's sake...
LADY. Apology accepted.

(ROSE smiles at LADY for a second.)

ROSE. Can you do that on cue... get all that riled up, and in turn get that kind of reaction out of others...
LADY. Not without cause.
ROSE. But if you had the right cause?
LADY. I suppose so. *(Pause.)* What?
ROSE. I, ah, think I could use your help...
LADY. You want me to help you? A few minutes ago...
ROSE. That was then.
LADY. You're awfully stubborn...
ROSE. And you're not? *(Pause.)* How else does anything ever get done?
LADY. I suppose so.
ROSE. You with me?

ROSE COLORED GLASS

LADY. As compared to what? Against you?
ROSE. I'd prefer to think of it as with me or without me.
LADY. And without me... you'd be?
ROSE. Nowhere, absolutely nowhere!
LADY. Then, we shall see... but for now... I'm in. And get some rest, you look terrible.
ROSE. Enough with this humbling business.

(LADY smiles and EXITS into her kitchen. PEG steps out from the shadows of the alley.)

PEG. And as December came, the lights still never went out over there.

(ROSE goes and gets an old typewriter, sets it down on the table, loads it with paper and begins to type. This typing is heard under the rest of PEG'S line. LADY is putting away a pen and paper.)

PEG. They were on when I went to bed and they were on when I got up... like a vigil... an eternal flame... a flame that could set the world on fire.....

(PEG crosses into LADY'S kitchen. LADY is making sausage.)

PEG. *(Cont'd.)* One room at a time...
LADY. Are you going to help me or not?
PEG. I was going to finish wrapping presents...
LADY. That can wait.
PEG. I was wrapping your Christmas present...
LADY. It can still wait...

ROSE COLORED GLASS

(PEG starts toward the door.)

LADY. Not till you're done helpin' me. Either load the hopper, or crank?
PEG. Crank. So, is that really pig gut?
LADY. Small intestine.
PEG. So you rip it's guts out, grind him up and then shove him into his own guts?
LADY. Why must you reduce everything down to its lowest common denominator?
PEG. What does that mean?
LADY. Stop thinking so much, it's only sausage.
PEG. It's sorta like he's eating himself...

(ROSE storms out into the alley and paces.)

ROSE. Public charge... now they are public charges... Public...

(ROSE turns to LADY'S kitchen door, looks at it, then storms in.)

ROSE. *(Cont'd.)* Public charges... now they are public charges!
LADY. Who?
ROSE. The children... public charges.
LADY. What? What's a public charge?
ROSE. Ward of the state, and I have to supply... This. *(SHE grabs a loaf of bread.)* No, no, half of this. *(SHE rips it apart, and slams it on the table.)* And this... *(SHE grabs a chunk of cheese.)* And a third of this... *(SHE grabs a sausage.)*

ROSE COLORED GLASS

LADY. Rose, my sausage. *(SHE grabs ROSE's hand before SHE hits the sausage on the table.)* Slow down. Now what...

ROSE. Three hundred and sixty five days a year, I have to come up with this...

(SHE goes for the bread, but LADY grabs her hand and holds it.)

LADY. Slowly...

ROSE. Three hundred and sixty five days a year... I have to guarantee our government that I can provide for this child...

LADY. But you can.

ROSE. Yes, but I must convince them that I can... so that he does not become a public charge... a financial burden to the people.

LADY. That's insane. How could he? You have a good business.

ROSE. But what if I should die, or the business goes under in these hard times?

LADY. The Society. The Society promised help once you find the child.

ROSE. It too, could go under, according to Mr. Fletcher...

PEG. Who's Mr. Fletcher?

ROSE. The undersecretary to the undersecretary to the undersecretary to the man who takes visa applications... who is taking his orders directly from your Mr. Roosevelt.

LADY. When did he become my Mr. Roosevelt?

ROSE. When he started keeping innocent little children out of this country based on... *(SHE grabs the sausage.)* On a technicality.

LADY. Rose, we haven't even found him yet...

ROSE COLORED GLASS

ROSE. And when we do, he will have a visa... and, no Mr. Roosevelt and his damn sausage law is going prevent me from doing so...

LADY. But...

ROSE. He has made it clear that he does not want these children in this country, and I am going to make it equally clear to him that...

LADY. That what?

ROSE. That he is wrong... damn it!

(SHE slaps the sausage in LADY'S hand, and storms out into the alley.)

LADY. Rose...

PEG. Is this that lowest denominator thing?

LADY. Yes. Go back to wrapping your presents. ROSE!

(ROSE is in the alley, pacing. LADY EXITS after ROSE. The lights dim on LADY'S kitchen and up on the alley.)

ROSE. Damn... It feels like I'm beating my head against a wall.

LADY. I...

ROSE. Here look at this... *(Pulling a piece of newspaper from her pocket.)* A 32 year old German Jewish doctor and his wife were not allowed into this country because they might become public charges. He had $1,600 cash, 3 letters of support and a sister claiming she owns $70,000 worth of property...

LADY. Then why wouldn't they grant him a visa?

ROSE. They said it wasn't enough. Was it because he is Jewish?

ROSE COLORED GLASS

LADY. Maybe. Maybe not.
ROSE. Maybe, maybe not. God, love me, or hate me... but just don't tell me you don't care.
LADY. Rose, surely God cares...
ROSE. I can't even find him to tell him I'm trying... I'm trying.

(A group of carolers are heard singing. IT CAME UPON A MIDNIGHT CLEAR ,THAT GLORIOUS SONG OF OLD... ROSE begins to hum along in anger. LADY joins in, to sing along to calm ROSE down. It does.)

LADY. *(Soothingly singing.)* OF ANGELS BENDING NEAR THE EARTH TO TOUCH THEIR HARPS OF GOLD. *(They are quiet, then...)* Rose Fleishman knows a Christmas carol?
ROSE. Rose Fleishman knows many things. What she doesn't know is what came upon a midnight clear...
LADY. A miracle.
ROSE. Miracles. Right.
LADY. Yes. Exactly. Like your Festival of Lights. See I know too... This Chanukah. Didn't some oil burn at some time for eight days? Wasn't that a miracle?
ROSE. You're talking ancient miracles. A new miracle... that's what it's going to take to get this boy because I don't seem to be doing any good...
LADY. You have to stop taking all this anger out on yourself.

(LADY reaches out and touches ROSE. ROSE pulls back.)

ROSE COLORED GLASS

ROSE. Don't.
LADY. Rose, I was only trying to...
ROSE. Don't!

(ROSE turns and goes into HER kitchen and stops at the door to the deli. LADY watches her, then turns and walks to the Pub kitchen door, then turns back to look at ROSE. Freeze. PEG ENTERS the alley.)

PEG. My grandmother had spent most of her life looking behind her, keeping track of my grandfather, my father, me... and the pain... the very thing that made her strive onward was also the thing she kept looking over her shoulder at...

(LADY turns toward the pub door and freezes. ROSE turns back and looks out to the alley toward the pub.)

PEG. *(Cont'd.)* And, I think Mrs. Fleishman needed someone who cared enough to look back at...

(ROSE turns away from the alley, as LADY turns back to look at ROSE.)

PEG. *(Cont'd.)*... at her.

(The lights fade on both doorways, and then on the alley.)

END OF ACT I

ROSE COLORED GLASS

ACT II

(The lights come up on the cold winter alley as the two women ENTER. ROSE rubs her arms to stay warm, as LADY tightens up her sweater.)

    ROSE. It's...
    LADY. Cold.
    ROSE. Yes... yes.
    LADY. Very.
    ROSE. Yes, very...
    BOTH. Would you like to...
    ROSE. I'm, ah...
    LADY. Yes...
    ROSE. Come for coffee. LADY. Come for tea.
    LADY. I have bread to get rising.
    ROSE. Then, I'll come for tea.

(ROSE and LADY move into LADY'S kitchen as PEG goes into the alley.)

    PEG. The pathway between the two kitchens was at least open, not overly traveled, but open. And the alley, and the world, seemed to be getting smaller. It was January 1939. Hitler's troops were marching across Europe, and not two steps ahead of him, the people of Europe were running. The few arms that were open to them... were quickly becoming within arms reach of the Nazis'...

(PEG steps into LADY'S kitchen.)

    LADY. I'll just put that bread to rising...
    PEG. You'd make a terrible Jew.
    LADY. With a name like O'Riley, I should think so.
    PEG. No, really Nanna. While you were waiting for the bread to rise, the Egyptians would have come in and beat you to a pulp.
    LADY. Aren't you late for school?
    PEG. It's true. It's called Passover. Nothing had yeast in it, so they didn't have to wait around... not that I'm sayin' you just sit around while it's rising but...
    LADY. Get.
    PEG. Okay, I'm going... but think about it...

(PEG EXITS.)

    LADY. What part of that are you telling her, and what part is she making up?
    ROSE. It's a fine line.
    LADY. And you wonder why you are misunderstood.
    ROSE. Am I? *(Pause.)* You've done a nice job raising her.
    LADY. I'm afraid she's actually raised herself.

(PEG REENTERS.)

    LADY. What'd you forget?

ROSE COLORED GLASS

PEG. Mail's early. I thought it'd be my mail order...
LADY. At 8 in the morning? You are not going to be late for school because of the mail.
ROSE. Mail order. You let her order lingerie?
PEG. Flannel nightgown.
ROSE. Good choice.
LADY. See? Raises herself. So, no mail order?
PEG. No, it's all for Mrs. Fleishman... two from London.

(ROSE grabs the mail from PEG.)

PEG. *(Cont'd.)* No return address. And one from the Children's Aid Fund.
LADY. See a little help from the Catholic ladies didn't kill you...
ROSE. I think I said thank you for the address several times.
LADY. I never get tired of hearing it...
PEG. Open the mystery one first.
ROSE. *(ROSE fumbles with the letter.)* Here, do this.

(PEG takes and opens the letter.)

PEG. It's not in English.
ROSE. *(Hopefully.)* Sabina! *(Reading.)* Meine Liebe Tante Rose...
PEG. In English... English.
ROSE. My Dearest Aunt *(Realizing.)* Rose. I am in England now living with a lady and her son... They are a nice family and very kind and generous to me. They have a wonderfully plump Welsh maid who wanted to wash everything the minute I got here. We traveled from Vienna at night with some

very kind people called Quakers. We stayed at a different house each day. I had to stay at one house for a week, because I tripped and broke my ankle when we were traveling one night. The doctor who set it said he did the best he could considering. I don't know what that meant, but it doesn't hurt as much now. So, when the maid went to wash my shirt she found a rip in the collar and when she went to fix it, she found sewn inside two pieces of a photograph with your address and a note from Mamma telling me to send it to you. So, I am.

(ROSE holds the photo halves together, but there is a gap in the middle.)

    PEG. Where's the rest of it?
    LADY. Rose?
    ROSE. Go get my music box.

(PEG EXITS.)

    ROSE. *(Reading.)* I am hoping to come to America some day soon, but I am told there is more to it than just getting on a boat. Is that true?
    LADY. Rose?
    ROSE. Look, it is my family. My sister and her husband in front of their home.

(PEG returns with the music box. ROSE takes the other piece and fits it into the photo.)

    ROSE. And Abraham. The building... they live on the second floor.

ROSE COLORED GLASS

LADY. But he is holding a suitcase...
ROSE. And my sister... she is holding her silver candlesticks.

(ROSE sits quietly and stares at the photo.)

LADY. That seems odd...
ROSE. They are leaving.
LADY. Perhaps it is just for that holiday?
ROSE. No. When you leave a place forever, you take what is most precious to you. You... you would take your Bible.
LADY. And some things of Paddy's.
ROSE. My sister... her candlesticks. *(Reading.)* I have not heard from Mamma or Papa since I left Vienna. I try not to think of the terrible things happening at home. *(To PEG.)* How easily we say that... *(Reading.)* I was told to tell you to write to me at the American embassy, for my own protection. There is a lot I do not understand. Please write to me soon. Your loving nephew, Abraham.

PEG. Do you think he's in London?
LADY. Rose, this is so exciting! *(ROSE is still.)* Rose?
ROSE. I am no closer than I was ten minutes ago.
LADY. You know he is alive and well and being taken care of... that's a hell of a lot closer than... *(To PEG.)* Will you get to school?
PEG. Certain things are more important.
LADY. Yes, and your mail order did not come... so scoot.
PEG. No, I mean this.
LADY. You can catch up after school.
PEG. Sure, after it's all been talked out.
ROSE. I will make latkes after school, and we will write

Abraham.

PEG. But it's not Chanukah...

ROSE. We will make an exception.

LADY. No, we will not be making an exception... in this house, young lady, you will not be rewarded for being late for school, or not doing homework... or sneaking out on chores.

PEG. Nanna!

LADY. I am serious... now, off to school or you will never see another...?

ROSE. Latke.

LADY. Latke, for as long as you live.

(PEG looks to ROSE, who motions her out.)

PEG. Oh... okay.

(PEG EXITS.)

ROSE. You are too hard on her.

LADY. Someone has to be. *(Pause.)* Latkes?

ROSE. Like Irish potatoes... only shredded with onion and...

LADY. More like hash browns. Only you boil them?

ROSE. We do not boil everything.

LADY. *(Pause.)* That's it? He's safe. No tears of joy... nothing?

ROSE. Safe? I don't know that. England is not so very far from Germany. If a little Austrian boy can get there, don't you think the Nazis can too? Suppose their airplanes come with bombs? Then how safe will he be?

LADY. Oh, Rose, that'll never happen.

ROSE. Suppose they don't like him and send him back... to

ROSE COLORED GLASS

an empty apartment?
LADY. You shouldn't get so carried away with your thinkin'.
ROSE. Here, open my head... you will see my mind is at ease. The tears of joy will come when he is sitting in my kitchen eating latkes.
LADY. And in your heart?
ROSE. I no longer have one.
LADY. I highly doubt that.
ROSE. At night... it is the worst. When I lie in bed and there is nothing to do but think. What if she is alive, what if she is not? What about Papa? Over and over. And now I see these silver candlesticks and I know that sleep will not come to me again for a very long time. *(Pause.)* The other letter, please.

(LADY begins to reach for ROSE.)

LADY. I'm sorry.
ROSE. I'm sure you are. The other letter.
LADY. Fine.

(ROSE holds out her hand, and LADY places the letter in it.)

ROSE. Dear Mrs. Fleishman... We received your letter of November, 1938.
LADY. That was over 5 months ago.
ROSE. Postal work, it's a government job.
LADY. Keep reading.
ROSE. Several ships filled with European children have arrived within the last year. Thank you for your full description. It is hard without a photo. Finding the boy is just the be-

ginning, getting him permission to live in the United States is another matter. I have forwarded your information to the American Consulate in London. I suggest that you contact them for help. The best of luck to you... Sincerely, Miss Razovsky, German Jewish Children's Aid.

LADY. Now, all we need is that highly elusive visa... and a boat.

(ROSE starts to EXIT.)

LADY. Where are you going?
ROSE. I have to... think.
LADY. I'm glad you found him.
ROSE. We... we found him. But getting him...
LADY. We will work very hard at that...

(ROSE EXITS into her kitchen as the lights fade on LADY'S kitchen and up on alley.)

PEG. The latkes were all but forgotten. The next three weeks...

(Lights up on both kitchens. We hear ROSE typing again.)

PEG. *(Cont'd.)* Mrs. Fleishman spent at that typewriter, and when not pounding away at the keys she was on the phone... to the Immigration Department, the Embassy in Washington, The Joint... all in search of that highly elusive visa.

(PEG crosses to ROSE'S mail box, takes out a large envelope, and takes it into ROSE.)

ROSE COLORED GLASS

PEG. Immigration Department.
ROSE. How could such a small boy require such a mound of paperwork?

(PEG moves back into the alley.)

PEG. And my grandmother kneaded bread... to death... trying to figure out how to get... a boat.

(Lights fade on kitchens. ROSE is typing.)

PEG. *(Cont'd.)* I never thought I would see the day they were both working on the same project... let alone together. They worked in their own ways... my grandmother was best with things she could touch, and knead, and pound, and stir and chop... and loaf. Mrs. Fleishman, on the other hand, was better with things you couldn't touch... ideas, schemes, plans ...

(Lights up on ROSE reading a letter.)

ROSE. Fine. If visitors visas are the easiest to obtain, what's to say that life is not just one big vacation? Ah, see section Five-B, what constitutes a vacation...

(Lights up on LADY'S kitchen. SHE is on the phone.)

LADY. Mr. Brown... what's to stop you from picking up one small boy after you unload your ship? You've got to come back here anyway... I should talk to who? Let me write that down. I see. Yes, Yes, I see...

ROSE COLORED GLASS

(Lights fade on the kitchens.)

PEG. They both had a long ways to go...

(Lights up on ROSE'S kitchen. ROSE is working on the letters, as LADY knocks on her door.)

LADY. I received a wire back today.
ROSE. And, what does it say?
LADY. I don't know. It is from a passenger line. I have been looking for a boat for Abraham... technically, passage on an ocean liner.
ROSE. I should hope so... I'm not ready to put him in the bottom of a turnip boat.
LADY. Good, because, I've tried that... it's against some sort of law.
ROSE. You're kidding? *(LADY smiles.)* I take it you're not. It's not that simple, you know.
LADY. I'm well aware... however, when it does become that simple, I thought it would save time to at least know what we can't do.
ROSE. Thank you. *(LADY shrugs it off.)* No, really.
LADY. *(Reading.)* Southampton Lines leave 1st every month. Stop. Arrive New York City 10 days. Stop. Passage paid in advance. Stop. All papers in order before departure. Stop. Immigration visa required. Stop. Good?

(ROSE goes to a stack of letters and papers.)

ROSE. I have to start at the beginning. Visa application...

ROSE COLORED GLASS

pages 1-10... the who, what, where, when.
    LADY. You know ten pages about this little boy?
    ROSE. And his family... and... and what I didn't have an answer for... I made up.
    LADY. You shouldn't make things up on government forms.
    ROSE. Incomplete applications will be returned...
    LADY. What did you make up?
    ROSE. I told them my sister was dead.
    LADY. That's a lie...
    ROSE. Is it? She sent him away for a reason. At best, to this government, she is no more than a statistic... a number... I will not let that stand in the way of my getting Abraham. And besides, it is a small lie... and we aren't even sure it is a lie...
    LADY. What else?
    ROSE. Thirteen pages guaranteeing he would not become a public charge.
    LADY. The sausage documents.
    ROSE. Including everything about the deli but my Gefilte fish recipe. Letters from the Hebrew Sheltering and Immigration Aid Society guaranteeing funds should the bottom drop out of Gefilte fish, a letter from my bank... To whom it may concern: this is to guarantee that the mortgage on Mrs. Hershel Fleishman's property at 311 72nd has been paid in full as of...
    LADY. Your mortgage is paid off?
    ROSE. For years. The price was right.
    LADY. So, I remember.
    ROSE. And that in savings and assets... well, that... who needs to know? Oh, and a letter from you saying he has an after school job at the pub.
    LADY. He's working for me?
    ROSE. You need the help... It was a last minute idea.

ROSE COLORED GLASS

LADY. I really would like to do my own hiring... what if he's not suited... what sort of experience...

ROSE. It's only on paper...

LADY. I'll remember that when he's sweeping my floors... you could have asked.

ROSE. You were busy.

LADY. You could have asked.

ROSE. I'm sorry. Next time, I'll ask.

LADY. And what if he just doesn't work out? I'm to let my neighbor's nephew go?

ROSE. I'm sorry.

LADY. I'm sure it will work out... you really should have...

ROSE. Asked. I should have asked.

LADY. Yes.

ROSE. I'm sorry but paper work takes time, and for everyday we do not have a visa, someone else is getting one, filling the quota of who can come here and if while we are waiting they should fill the quota...

LADY. You would have to wait another year?

ROSE. Yes, and again take the chance of being one of the few.

LADY. No visitor's visas?... no...

ROSE. No. I would have been better off if my sister had sent him to Brazil or Cuba. From there they will take immigrants.

LADY. So, why can't you reroute him?

ROSE. What? Put him on a boat to Cuba?

LADY. That, perhaps, stops in New York on the way back...

ROSE. No. Ideas like that are just too far-fetched.

LADY. Are they?

ROSE. Don't... just don't.

ROSE COLORED GLASS

LADY. Don't what?
ROSE. Get me thinking in that direction.
LADY. You apply for a visa through Cuba, and he comes to the United States.
ROSE. And while I am redoing all this paperwork... what? He so much as steps off the boat, who knows, he could have to stay six months. Besides, I don't know anyone in Cuba... they too, would need guarantees that he will be taken care of there... What, he lives in a hut and works in a cigar factory?
LADY. Hut? Cigar factory? Where do you get your vision of the world?
ROSE. National Geographic... and that is a crazy idea.
LADY. We're not getting anywhere with the sane ideas.
ROSE. It is a crazy idea... even for you.

(Lights fade on ROSE'S kitchen, as LADY returns to her kitchen. Lights fade up on the alley.)

PEG. A bit far-fetched but wasn't Cuba sorta the back door to America, and who said you always had to enter through the front door? And, somehow, it was the thought of having him just that much closer that warranted giving any time at all to this farfetched idea. So, for the next few days they went about their silent business...

(Lights up low on both kitchens.)

PEG. *(Cont'd.)* And every so often they would look up from stuffing sausage or making soup to stare blankly into space, frown, then madly return to the typewriter, or a note pad and write with the frantic speed of someone whose life depended upon those thoughts, in the right order... all working towards a solution... that became vaguer the more they attempted to make it clearer... and they kept at it... until one of them just couldn't stand it anymore.

(Lights up on LADY'S kitchen. SHE is on the phone.)

LADY. Could I have the number for the Cuban Embassy in Washington, DC, please.

(Lights fade on LADY and up on ROSE. ROSE types.)

PEG. *(With a newspaper.)* And so they waited... in a world where everything seemed balanced on a very tight rope... Hitler's troops had taken Prague. And the Nazi reign of terror was spreading like wildfire across Czechoslovakia. Ignoring the agreement made at the Munich conference, Hitler broke his promise to England not to invade Czechoslovakia. The fact that no country stood up to stop the spreading terror, gave Hitler permission to continue... Hitler declared that history would remember him as the greatest German of all time.

(Lights slowly fade up on ROSE. SHE places a linen napkin on her head and lights the Sabbath candles. SHE begins to sing the blessing.)

ROSE. Baruch-atah adonoy, eloheinu melech h'alom, asher....

(SHE then abruptly stops, blows the candles out. SHE looks toward LADY'S and in frustration and disillusionment EX-

ROSE COLORED GLASS

ITS to LADY'S kitchen. Lights up on LADY who is cutting out newspaper articles.)

ROSE. What are you doing?
LADY. Clipping things of interest...
ROSE. The daily reports of the Intergovernmental Committee... what else?
LADY. Letters to the editor urging United States involvement in the plight of European Jews... and this one, which is signed by the owner of a local Pub and Grill.
ROSE. I asked.
LADY. Very well written... almost articulate.
ROSE. I asked.
LADY. True, and it is a far sight easier than paying a boy from now till he graduates Harvard.
ROSE. How often is that going to come up...
LADY. Consider the subject dropped... until such time when I deem it necessary to...
ROSE. Why are you doing this, anyway?
LADY. Has Mrs. Roosevelt answered your letter?
ROSE. What do you think?
LADY. Yes, yes. American apathy... give the soapbox the day off. I thought perhaps a well-written, sympathetic letter from an Irish American...
ROSE. Complete with a press packet?
LADY. I thought it might help.
ROSE. And, what will it say?
LADY. Dear Mrs. Roosevelt...
ROSE. And?
LADY. And, you should trust me. At least I asked.
ROSE. Told.

ROSE COLORED GLASS

LADY. Is there a difference, to you? What do you hear from Cuba?

ROSE. They would just as soon not be involved.

LADY. Who did you talk to?

ROSE. An assistant to the Ambassador, a Mr. Rodriguiz. I could hardly understand him.

LADY. You should have let me talk to him.

ROSE. What? With the daily flow of Latins coming into the pub...

LADY. That's not what I meant. What did he tell you?

ROSE. That immigration matters, especially those requesting special visas or permits, would have to be handled through proper government channels...

LADY. So?

ROSE. So, I called Rabbi Schulman...

LADY. Rabbi Schulman is a proper government channel?

ROSE. THINKING... perhaps a Rabbi might have a little more clout, and he went round and round with them, to find out that if Abraham stayed on the boat, he still needs an American Visa, if he got off the boat, he could have a visa from Cuba... after 12 months in the country.

LADY. Close, but no cigar?

ROSE. That's not funny.

LADY. *(Long pause.)* Dear Mrs. Roosevelt...

ROSE. That's not going to help. I know that, you know that...

LADY. No, Rose, I don't know that.

ROSE. Well, maybe it's time you did. Face it; we aren't going to get the boy.

LADY. You're giving up, all of a sudden?

ROSE. You have given up on your son and you are still

ROSE COLORED GLASS

living.
LADY. Living yes, quitting, no!
ROSE. I don't see you trying to get him home...
LADY. He could come home if he wanted to.
ROSE. Exactly. He has a choice.
LADY. Rose! Stop right there... you're crossin' a line...
ROSE. Your son won't come home and you've given up trying to get him here.
LADY. Wait a minute. Just because I don't ramble on and on about it and make it the focus of my whole existence doesn't mean I'm not trying. You haven't seen me march into your kitchen and yell about quittin' anything, have ya'?
ROSE. Well, maybe it's time you did... what we are doing here is useless! You think writing a letter to Mrs. Roosevelt is going to help us get Abraham? How absurd is that? Or do you need a million or so government officials to tell us... to tell you how stupid you are... how insane... how totally ridiculous this whole idea is... how...

(ROSE goes, grabs the letter, crumples it up and throws it at LADY.)

LADY. How desperate you are...
ROSE. Yes. And, I refuse to live life as some desperate, old...
LADY. So you give up?
ROSE. Yes, and so should you...
LADY. No! You do not walk in here and dictate to me...
ROSE. Why not? What? You think someone is sitting in the White House reading these crazy letters that are postmarked from a run down pub on the south side of Chicago. What world

do you live in? Face it, you're a poor immigrant and nobody here in America wants any more of you. No one cares about you or me or Abraham or Sabina or Papa. No one! Give it up.

LADY. No.

ROSE. Are you blind? Don't you get it? Nobody is saving anybody!

LADY. Yes they are.

ROSE. Who?

LADY. Me! I'm saving me!

ROSE. What?? Is that what this is about?... this whole charade of friendship? Soothing your soul for your son? Or for your husband? Well, you can relax. God won't be disappointed in you anymore!

LADY. Don't talk to me about God. At least I believe in knowing when I need help... and asking for it... which is more than I can say about you!

ROSE. I'll take it when it comes without strings attached.

(ROSE EXITS in a huff.)

LADY. Without strings... huh! Who the hell do you have to be to help Rose Fleishman? The King of England?

(LADY notices the letter on the floor. SHE picks it up and EXITS into the pub. A beat. SHE comes back in.)

LADY. *(Calling after ROSE.)* And for your information, God and I are just fine. Charade, huh? *(Picking up the pen.)* Like we can't do better than that!

(LADY then picks up a bottle of booze and EXITS again. Lights

ROSE COLORED GLASS

fade on LADY'S kitchen and up on the alley. PEG is kicking rocks.)

PEG. We could do better than that! And there was no way we were going to give up... not now. The way I figured it, I was at least two steps ahead of them... no really. For instance... *(A switch to younger PEG.)* He will look European... which will make Mrs. Fleishman happy... but that will have to change. He needs to look American... dress like the rest of us. The V-neck shirt will have to go, ours button all the way down, and the flat cap will never do... baseball cap. *(SHE picks up the rock and tosses it in the air.)* And that's another thing, he will have to learn how to play baseball... stick ball at first. I could teach him right here in the alley... He would stand down there... *(SHE takes "him" down to the far end of the alley.)* And I would pitch from here... cause there's less chance of breaking a window from here... Oh, and that's another thing I'd have to warn him about is how mad everyone gets when you break a window... Then I pitch real slow... Ah, but first I'd have to show him how to hold the stick. You hold it down here, one fist up from the bottom of the stick and you plant your feet apart like this. But you don't lean over the plate too far, or stand back too far... kinda in the middle, like this. And you can't stand like a girl, although I really don't know what that means... I guess we'll know it when we see it... and then I'll pitch. Nice and easy. *(SHE runs back to her side of the alley, and pitches to him.)* And on the first try... no... on the third try... I throw a perfect pitch, and you hit the ball and it goes way over my head, and out of the alley into the street... and right smack into the side of Clancey's milk truck... and I'd laugh and yell, "Sorry Mr. Clancey, he's not from around here," and he'd yell back the same thing he's been yellin' since

ROSE COLORED GLASS

I was born... "Twenty-five years ago stunts like that woulda killed my horse."... and then we'd both laugh... I might have to teach you the American sense of humor too... nobody said this could happen overnight. And I'd teach you how to pitch but for that we have to go to the park... I got a lot of power battin', my accuracy needs a little... well, let's just say there are less windows in the park. *(SHE begins kicking the rock again.)* Oh, and I'll have a whole lot of explaining to do about the concept of the blue plate special... it's not real clear to me either... and I'll show you how to get to places. In Chicago there are short cuts to everything but school and the library. *(SHE sits on the crate.)* And then there is food... that is a whole day's lesson. Maybe we could figure out why watermelon only appears in the summer... I wish you'd hurry up and get here...

(ROSE ENTERS the alley.)

ROSE. *(To PEG.)* And what are you doing out here... dreaming the afternoon away?
PEG. Maybe.
ROSE. I suppose someone has to...

(ROSE EXITS to her kitchen.)

PEG. It wasn't as if she'd given up, but how often can you be told no... the weeks drug on slowly, and she still continued the struggle, only quietly. My grandmother, on the other hand, had decided to place the whole thing in God's hands, a Catholic God, however, and prayed for that one...
LADY. Isolated incident.
PEG. That would somehow turn this whole thing around.

ROSE COLORED GLASS

And she... and we... tried not to be affected by our friend's new distance... no matter how lonely it was beginning to get...

(LADY ENTERS the alley, stops short of ROSE'S door, then begins to return to her kitchen. LADY is surprised to find ROSE down the alley.)

    ROSE. Oh, I, ah... fresh air...
    LADY. What's that smell?
    ROSE. It's Tuesday.
    LADY. Ah, blue plate Borscht... good choice. *(ROSE smiles.)* How are things with you?
    ROSE. The same. *(Pause.)* I have heard nothing from abroad.
    LADY. I have been meaning to drop in...

(The phone rings at ROSE'S.)

    ROSE. So have I... there have just been things on my mind.

(The phone rings.)

    LADY. Your telephone is ringing.
    ROSE. I have missed our morning teas...
    LADY. Aren't you going to pick that up? *(The phone rings again.)* Rose, it's your phone in there jinglin' off the hook.
    ROSE. *(Pause.)* Oh, all right. *(ROSE goes into her kitchen and picks up the phone.)* Yes, Yes, this is Mrs. Fleishman. This is who? Yes, yes just a moment please. *(Yelling to LADY.)* Come in here quickly.
    LADY. What?

ROSE COLORED GLASS

(LADY ENTERS the deli.)

ROSE. It is the secretary to Mrs. Roosevelt. A man... a Mr. Coleman.

LADY. I can't picture men typing.

ROSE. Shh. Yes, yes. Yes, Mr. Coleman, she is my neighbor. Yes, my nephew Abraham, but he is only one of many... we have tried all conventional avenues. Yes, yes, I'll hold. *(To LADY.)* You actually wrote the letter?

LADY. Letters.

(ROSE takes a beat, as she realizes what LADY has done.)

ROSE. How many?

LADY. A few... dozen, maybe...

ROSE. What did you write about?

LADY. The same thing that you wrote about only with more heart.

ROSE. More heart?

LADY. That sentimental side you steer way from all the time.

ROSE. I can be just as... all right, all right, maybe not...

LADY. What are you waiting for?

ROSE. To talk to Mrs. Roosevelt...

LADY. You're going to talk to Eleanor Roosevelt?

ROSE. Oh... I had better sit down. I need to pull myself together.

LADY. Don't worry. I told her all about you.

ROSE. Wonderful. Now I have to pull myself together in the image you created of me... which was what? *(Into phone.)*

ROSE COLORED GLASS

Yes. Yes. Speaking. Hello, Mrs. Roosevelt. *(To LADY.)* It's Mrs. Roosevelt. *(Into phone.)* Yes, I'll try...
    LADY. What? She wants you to call her Eleanor?
    ROSE. Shhhhh.

(PEG ENTERS from the alley.)

    PEG. Who's she talking to?
    LADY. The First Lady.
    PEG. Mrs. Roosevelt?!
    LADY. Yes... shhhhh.
    PEG. Right, and the next is we'll be walking on the moon.
    LADY. SHHHHHHH!!
    PEG. All right, all right.

(PEG EXITS to alley.)

    PEG. No, it turns out it was true... she was actually talking to Eleanor Roosevelt. THE Eleanor Roosevelt. A woman with many causes... and all of a sudden we were a cause.
    ROSE. It's not just the nephew of mine, but hundreds of children. Yes, yes, I'm familiar with the Wagner bill...
    PEG. *(Still in the alley.)* A bill in Congress asking for US acceptance of 20,000 refugee children outside the quotas...
    LADY. Yes, yes... we read... we clip.
    PEG. And all of a sudden we had the ear of someone who was supposed to listen... who really wanted to listen...
    ROSE. I am afraid you do not understand the severity of my situation...
    LADY. Rose, remember you are speaking to Mrs. Roosevelt!

ROSE COLORED GLASS

ROSE. I'm sorry... Mrs. Roosevelt... I know you understand, but it is not as if you would be taking in orphans. They all have homes and we have made arrangements for funding... yes, but if they are not allowed to enter this country, they will be stuck in Europe *(Pause.)* Yes, he's Jewish. *(Long pause.)* Yes. Mrs. Roosevelt, I know things take time, but...

PEG. There was a long silence... and then like a fine tuned machine the work began... my grandmother sorted through records, found addresses as Mrs. Fleishman fed answers to almost a year's worth of work to Mrs. Roosevelt.

ROSE. Yes, yes. Ten months ago... no, no... but the quota of permanent immigrants from Germany has not been filled for this year and yet we are still waiting for the visa. But it is only 27,000 to begin with... Yes, yes, Southampton Lines. *(To LADY.)* Give me that. *(In the phone.)* Yes. A Mr. Grady, New York City. Yes. Funds are available. Mrs. Roosevelt, they just need permission to get on the boat... yes, I understand. *(Pause.)* Mrs. Roosevelt... thank you.

(SHE slowly hangs up the phone.)

LADY. So... So?
ROSE. So, she will take it to the President.
LADY. Oh...
ROSE. No, not just an "oh"... I got someone to listen to me. Someone who can change things. No, you... got someone to listen. And I'm... so... *(A pause as ROSE looks at LADY.)*

(Lights fade out on ROSE'S kitchen and up on the alley.)

PEG. To us Mrs. Roosevelt was a woman of her word. She

ROSE COLORED GLASS

did talk to the President... and to the American Embassy... and to Southampton Lines... specifically to a Mr. Grady, who was more than happy to help his country especially since business had been down over the last year or so... And what had taken Mrs. Fleishman and my grandmother and me almost a year to begin, Mrs. Roosevelt finished in less than a month...

(Lights fade up on LADY'S kitchen. PEG is kneading bread.)

PEG. So, what I want to know... is how come it took you so long? Mrs. Roosevelt knew just who to call...

LADY. She's married to the President.

PEG. So?

LADY. So... they go to a lot of parties, know a lot of people...

PEG. You think she talked to people about helping Mrs. Fleishman at a party?

LADY. Maybe... maybe not.

PEG. How do you think she knew who to call?

LADY. She knows a lot... good God, child, can't you be satisfied that Mrs. Roosevelt is helping?

PEG. A real spy is never truly satisfied... perhaps if I ordered a trench coat from the mail order catalogue, it might be easier for me to find stuff out. I mean Mrs. Roosevelt can't know everyone and everything in this country... nobody can know everything.

LADY. I know a 14 year old Irish girl who thinks she can...

PEG. Nanna.

LADY. There are a lot of people who are specialists who work for the President.

PEG. That's it! And there might be one man who specializes in knowing who to call, in case the President needs to talk to... a specialist.

LADY. Perhaps.

PEG. So that's who she called... the man who knows who to call.

LADY. I'm sure there was more to it than that.

PEG. Yeah... maybe. You know we're out of raisins.

LADY. You know, you're not making cinnamon rolls.

PEG. Oh. Do you think Mrs. Roosevelt will be at the boat?

LADY. That would be nice... but we're not going to get our hopes up. She's a busy lady.

PEG. Mrs. Fleishman thinks she'll be there... because of politics.

LADY. Politics?

PEG. Mrs. Fleishman says you vote for people who care about you. If Mrs. Roosevelt was at the boat, it would show us that she cared.

LADY. And, what does Mrs. Fleishman think about the president?

PEG. She wishes he cared more.

LADY. That's putting it mildly.

PEG. That's how she tells me things... not the way she tells you. What are we gonna do after we pick up Abe... for fun in New York?

LADY. We?

PEG. You, me and Mrs. Fleishman.

LADY. You, young lady, will be in school.

PEG. How come I can't go? I helped.

LADY. And we are very thankful... but you are not going to take time off from school just to go running off to New York City.

PEG. But, you're taking time off work.

ROSE COLORED GLASS

LADY. We are adults...

PEG. I'm old enough.

LADY. ... who can afford to pay extra help for a few days.

PEG. Then if I could come up with the money...

LADY. Peggy Jean O'Riley, don't even think about paying someone to go to school for you.

PEG. I still don't understand why I can't go...

LADY. Because New York City is... I will have enough to look after with Abraham and Rose. It is too much for me to think about... having to take care of a third person...

PEG. But I want to go... please.

LADY. No, and stop pouting. You look like you've just lost your best friend.

PEG. Maybe I have.

LADY. Oh, for heavens sake, child, wasn't that your plan all along that we become friends?

PEG. That was before I knew anyone was going to New York City.

(Lights fade down on LADY'S kitchen as PEG EXITS to alley.)

PEG. Nearly three months would go by as the final preparations were being made. In July Senator Wagner withdrew his bill. There would be no extra 20,000 children. The American Legion didn't like the bill, it would be a mistake, saying "that it was traditional American Policy that home life should be preserved, and that breaking up families, would be done by the proposed legislation." I guess they figured it was better for a family to stay together in a concentration camp than to send its children to freedom in the United States. But thanks to Mrs.

ROSE COLORED GLASS

Roosevelt there would be one boy...

(ROSE, with suitcase sitting on table, stares into space as LADY ENTERS ROSE'S kitchen with her suitcase.)

ROSE. You are early.
LADY. You packed?
ROSE. Yes. I should pack something to eat... for the train ride back.
LADY. I did. A potato salad, kippers and a tin fruit.
ROSE. I should throw in real food... the boy... *(SHE smiles at LADY.)* I... that will be fine. Thank you. I have never been to...
LADY. Me neither.
ROSE. You look a little nervous.
LADY. Me? No. Now you... you look a little nervous.
ROSE. Do I?
LADY. A little.
ROSE. You look a little nervous... too.
LADY. It is just that you and I have never traveled together...
ROSE. We have practically lived together for the last six months, it will be like that... only on wheels. *(ROSE opens her bag, and looks again.)* I just hope I have everything.
LADY. You got the jacket?
ROSE. Packed. But I will check again.
LADY. If it's packed, it's packed.
ROSE. I hope it fits.
LADY. It will fit.
ROSE. Boys grow a lot. He's at that age... who knows when that picture was taken?
LADY. It will be fine.

ROSE COLORED GLASS

ROSE. What if he looks like his father, tall and thin...

LADY. It will be fine.

ROSE. The shoulders... that is how you tell a poorly made jacket. What if the shoulders are too big...

LADY. It will be...

ROSE. I just hope I packed everything.

LADY. It is only over night. If we need something, we shall buy it.

ROSE. With the prices in New York City?

LADY. We will treat ourselves. *(Pause.)* What do you want to do first... in the city?

ROSE. I will hug him and hold him.

LADY. After all that?

ROSE. We will find a good deli. He's been in that country for over a year... he's probably thin as a rail or worse, all that starch...We will need a street map.

LADY. I won't let you get lost.

ROSE. You have never been to New York City...

LADY. We will get a street map...

ROSE. I just hope I have everything packed...

LADY. And I hope we arrive a bit early... so we can find a good Irish pub and you can have a few pints before you go pick up this young man... otherwise he may take one look at this nervous hen of an aunt he has and get right back on the boat.

ROSE. Me? I'm not the one that packed her pantry in case we get stuck someplace in the middle of nowhere...

LADY. And when we do... a lot of good that map of yours will do you.

ROSE. I've had your kippers... I'm better off with the map.

LADY. Fine. Be that way. *(SHE EXITS to the alley.)* If you can Gefilte a fish...

ROSE COLORED GLASS

ROSE. Yes. Yes. I can...
LADY. Loaf a salmon. Are you coming?
ROSE. Yes.

(LADY EXITS to the alley, ROSE begins to follow her, turns back, goes to her music box, takes out the photo of Abraham, puts it into her purse, then hurries out into the alley.)

LADY. You'd really prefer the map over my kippers?
ROSE. Only in the middle of nowhere... *(Pause.)* Aren't you a... a little scared?
LADY. A little nervous yes, scared... a little... for you. I'm scared that he won't be what you want... what you expect.
ROSE. I don't know what that is...
LADY. A living part of your sister.
ROSE. He is that.
LADY. But if he is not how you remember her?
ROSE. He will be... either way, I will love him as she would have wanted me to. *(Pause.)* But if we don't go, we will spend the day at the train station... with your kippers.
LADY. God forbid.

(ROSE and LADY EXIT. PEG steps out into the alley and opens first her mail box, finding nothing, then ROSE'S, from which SHE removes a letter and returns to the pub.)

(ROSE and LADY REENTER into a dock area. It is night. Sounds of the dock are heard.)

ROSE. Perhaps it is just late.
LADY. Check the time again.

ROSE COLORED GLASS

ROSE. I have read that cable a million times.
LADY. But, perhaps.
ROSE. It is just late. If trains can be late, imagine a boat...
PEG. *(Reading the letter.)* September 3, 1939. My Dearest Aunt Rose, Mrs. Deardon, our maid, helped me write this letter in English. We have been trying to contact you again by wire or long distance telephone for two days.
LADY. It is getting late, Rose... and there is nobody here.
ROSE. We will wait.
LADY. Perhaps it landed at another dock...
ROSE. It is supposed to be here.
PEG. All lines are tied up since England declared war on Germany Friday.
LADY. I am going... I'm going to find out where the boat is...

(LADY EXITS.)

PEG. We went and paid for my ticket aboard the Southampton early last week even though I still had my final visa interview on Friday. Mrs. Deardon said we could all relax once I had the ticket in my hand.

(LADY REENTERS.)

LADY. Rose, the boat... it arrived... it's over there.
ROSE. We must go.
LADY. Rose...
ROSE. Where is Abraham?
LADY. Rose...
PEG. We went to the interview on Friday. She told me to

ROSE COLORED GLASS

walk in quickly, stand up tall and try very hard not to limp because of my broken ankle. When I got there the officials asked me more questions and I know I answered them all right because he told me my papers were in order and it looked like I would be getting on that ship tomorrow. I just had to go through a simple physical exam.

ROSE. Come... we must find him... we must go.

(ROSE struggles to go. LADY stops her.)

LADY. Rose... listen to me. He never got on the boat.

PEG. The doctor was an older man, and he looked me over, and then he asked me to walk across the room. I did the best I could, but I guess it was not good enough. When he came back he told me and Mrs. Deardon that he could not pass me on the physical exam... on the grounds that I was likely to become a public charge.

ROSE. There must be some mistake. Why? Did you ask them why?

LADY. Some were not let on the boat because they were sick... or their papers were not in order or...

ROSE. Or what? What about Abraham?

LADY. Crippled. The ships roster shows that his ticket was sold to an Alex Beebe because Abraham's visa was denied... because he was likely to become a public charge...

ROSE. No, NO! I took care of all that. I took care of everything.

LADY. We will try again... We will talk to Mrs. Roosevelt... we will...

ROSE. Try again? So they can tell us what? We don't care. Nobody cares...

ROSE COLORED GLASS

LADY. Someone cares...

ROSE. The President doesn't care...the Congress doesn't... the newspapers...the churches. God doesn't care!

LADY. God does care...

ROSE. Then where is this God? He is certainly not looking after a little boy... It is... just a broken ankle... how can a government be so cruel... I just want my little boy...

LADY. Rose...

ROSE. He is my sister's son... He is supposed to be with me... he is supposed to grow up here... He is my sister's boy. I want Abraham... I want my little boy... It's a mistake.

LADY. *(Overlapping ROSE.)* We will try again. We will find a way. We will talk to Mrs. Roosevelt...

ROSE. It's all a big mistake. He is supposed to be with me... he is supposed to... I am supposed to raise him... Oh, Lady, I am supposed to...

LADY. *(Overlapping ROSE'S speech and then pulling ROSE to her.)* We will try again... we will not give up...

PEG. I was told I can appeal this action, and there are other special forms I need to fill out... and my ankle will surely get better, and I will learn how to walk so that I do not limp... I hope you get this letter before you leave for New York. I am sorry, Aunt Rose... I hug you with all my heart... Abraham. *(To the audience.)* The world an ocean away they had come so close to touching, now seemed even further away than before. What happened across an alley... the gentle grasp of each other's hand had held them together. But the belief and the faith that if you could just hold onto the hand of the world... everything would be all right, was gone... had slipped quietly from their grasp, from all our grasps. In a few days I would be turning 15, and he would be turning 13, celebrating his Bar Mitzvah in a world very far from here... I was allowed to grow up holding their hands... he was thrown into a world just out of their reach... but never out of their love.

ROSE. *(Quietly.)* He is only one boy.
PEG. He was only one boy... but he was our boy.

(Lights fade to black.)

END OF PLAY

ROSE COLORED GLASS

PROP LIST

Lady
Salmon Loaf in pan
Plates
Mugs and glasses
Bread bowl with dough
Silverware
Tea towels
Milk bottles-2
Apron
Tea cups with saucers-3
Teapot
Sugar bowl with sugar
Bookkeeping ledger
Pencils
Pad of note paper
1930's telephone
Rosary
Photo of Paddy on wall
Whiskey bottles
Shot glass
Piece of paper with address on it
Stationary
Sausage grinder
Bowl with sausage ingredients
Plate with sausage
Round loaves of bread-2
Block of cheese
Newspaper clippings
Scissors

96
Telegram
Suitcase
Rose
Broom
Candlesticks
Apron
Plate with gefilte fish
Silverware
Napkins
Tea towels-2
Bread bowl with strudel dough
Cookie sheet/baking pan
Knife
Piece of photograph-Abraham
Music box
Short wave radio
Telephone
Typewriter
Paper
Envelopes
Sheet of paper containing lists of government agencies
Plate with strudel
Typed letters - 7 - listed below
    Hebrew Sheltering and Immigration Society
    Council on Human Rights
    Department of Social Services
    2 generic claiming it is "not their department"
    1 generic claiming it is "not their problem"
    Immigration papers-Section 7-C Immigration Act
Newspaper clippings

ROSE COLORED GLASS

Pieces of photographs-Sabina, Karl
Letter from Hebrew Immigration
Letter from Bank
Letter from Lady
National Geographic Magazine
Candles
Box matches
Linen napkin
Suitcase with boy's jacket inside

Peg
School books
Alley rocks
Letters in Mail boxes - listed below
Sabina letter #1 with sections blacked out
Water bill
Sabina letter #2 with Hitler stamp, photograph of Abe
Letter unable to deliver
Birthday card
Large envelope with immigration/visa application
Abraham letter #1 with photos of Karl and Sabina
Letter from German Jewish Children's Aid Society
Abraham letter #2

PROP CLOTHES FOR SUITCASE
Boy's jacket
Slip
Sweater
Nightgown

ROSE COLORED GLASS

COSTUME PLOT

ROSE

Dress (everyday)
Slip
Earrings
Shoes
Stockings
2 Aprons (Act I, Act II)
Cardigan sweater
Handbag
Handkerchief
Dress (go to New York)
Hat (go to New York)
Gloves (go to New York)
Coat (go to New York)

LADY

Dress
Slip
Socks
Necklace (cross)
Shoes
Sweater (Paddy's)
2 Aprons (Act I, Act II)
Handbag (go to New York)
Handkerchief
Gloves (go to New York)
Hat (go to New York)
Coat (go to New York)

ROSE COLORED GLASS

PEG

Blouse
Pleated skirt
Slip
Socks
Saddle shoes
Barrette
Sweater
Coat
Apron

SOUND EFFECTS

Shortwave radio static
Shortwave radio announcer
Christmas carolers
Telephone rings
Dock sounds

ROSE COLORED GLASS

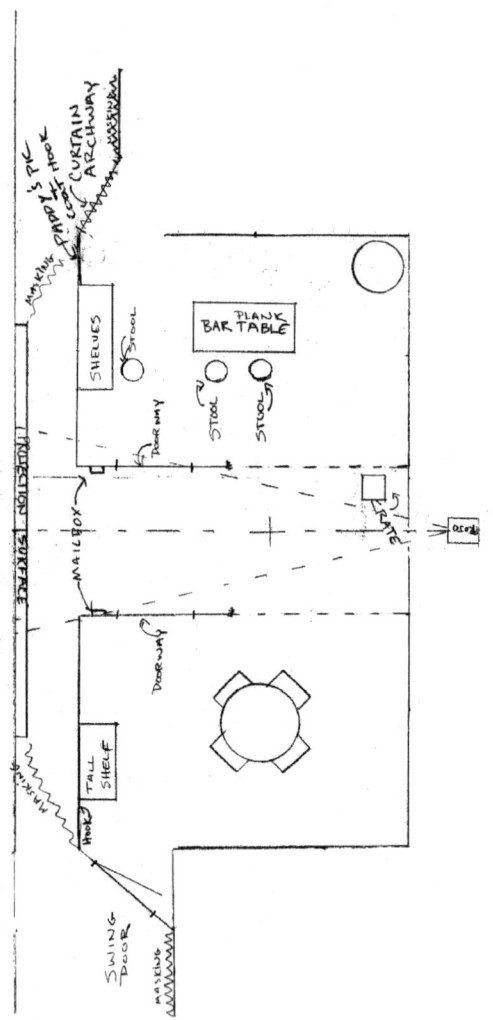

ROSE COLORED GLASS
3/4 Thrust
with projections

www.ingramcontent.com/pod-product-compliance
Lightning Source LLC
Chambersburg PA
CBHW070645300426
44111CB00013B/2276